CW00539231

THE BALANCE OF EXCELLENCE

Published in the UK in 2022 by Carl Klemm Publishing

Copyright © Carl Klemm 2022

Carl Klemm has asserted his right under
the Copyright, Designs and Patents Act, 1988,
to be identified as the author of this work.

All rights reserved. No part of this book may be reproduced,
stored in a retrieved system or transmitted, in any form
or by any means, electronic, mechanical, scanning, photocopy-
ing, recording or otherwise, without the prior permission of the
author and publisher.

Paperback ISBN 978-1-7399992-0-9

eBook ISBN 978-1-7399992-1-6

Cover design and typeset by SpiffingCovers.com

THE BALANCE OF EXCELLENCE

The blueprint for leaders of organisations and those supporting them in the pursuit of performance excellence

CARL KLEMM

FORMER HEAD OF TOYOTA PLANTS

FOREWORD

This is a great book that shows top management their role in implementing highly effective management methods in any region of the globe.

Carl is a trusted colleague of mine and has worked with me to develop the scientific approach to Built-in Quality in Process and has many years of practical experience in introducing management methods, which maximise the power of total engagement, development and teamwork, to all levels and in many types of organisation.

Shinichi Sasaki

Former Vice President of Toyota Motor Corporation

President of the Union of Japanese Scientists and Engineers

President of the International Academy for Quality

Picture taken in January 2010, when starting as
President and CEO of Toyota Motor Manufacturing Poland

Picture taken in March 2021 for
International Association for Quality Conference in Switzerland

ABOUT THE AUTHOR

- 50 years in automotive manufacturing.
- 25 years in Toyota. Retired after 11 years as the head of Toyota plants.
- 6 years in consulting for many and varied organisations.

Carl worked in manufacturing in the automotive industry for 50 years. Starting as a 5-year engineering apprentice with Vauxhall Motors (General Motors in the UK) and ending the last 6 years as president and CEO of Toyota Motor Manufacturing Poland.

Many years were spent in Quality and Production. He was able to work directly with hundreds of supplier companies and also with similar numbers of distributors and dealerships, throughout the world.

He has long harboured an ambition to support as many organisations as possible to benefit from Toyota's excellent practices.

In line with his ambition, whilst head of the Toyota Deeside plant in North Wales, Carl founded the Toyota Lean Management Centre (TLMC). The centre is based in the plant and is operated by Toyota members. It provides the opportunity for any organisation to see, question, learn and practise the methods Toyota operates in a working facility. The centre has supported more than 450 organisations since its inception in 2008.

Since retiring from Toyota, Carl has directly supported many and varied organisations and continues to do so.

PREFACE

I swore never to write this book!

The skills and requirements of good leadership and management cannot be learned just by academic study, only by using the methods and learning from practical experience. Continually delivering better and better performance by increasing the power of one's organisation and getting all that power moving in the correct direction and focused on the right priorities is what I mean by good leadership and management.

But, after 5 years of supporting a wide range of organisations, as a consultant, I learned three things which run as a common thread throughout them all.

1. The speed, extent and sustainability of progress in any organisation depends almost entirely upon the ownership and actions of us, its top management team.
2. The top management teams of all organisations get to where we are by doing the things we do now. This naturally gives us confidence in our own methods and concepts.
3. In order to invest the time and energy in changing the things we do, top management need to see the whole picture, and we need to be able to judge for ourselves before actually starting the journey.

So I have tried to present the whole picture in a way which explains how all of the many practical and cultural elements of good management fit together and in which order.

Each element has been explained in essence. Sufficiently to enable top management members to understand what is necessary and how and why it works, and enough to get started on the journey with some confidence.

Each element is a study topic on its own, but this can only be learned by doing, learning from experience, and by taking support from expert resources when necessary.

At the age of 40, I moved from an organisation, led and managed in what is sometimes called the typical Western command-and-control manner, to Toyota, which was led and managed quite differently. The transition was not an easy one. The biggest hurdles were putting my ego to one side and being ready to unlearn many of the things I held to be self-evident truths.

Was it smooth? No! It was the school of hard knocks. Admittedly, I was never a fast learner, but also Toyota strongly believes in everyone figuring things out for themselves. In this way, each concept and method becomes your own.

How long did it take? It took me 5 years to put the basic picture together. Since then, for the last 25 years, the learning has never stopped.

So, I have finally written this first book with the purpose of helping top management members to begin with putting the framework in place and thereby getting a flying start.

If you do decide to start and stick with the journey, I promise that your organisation will reach previously unimaginable levels of achievement!

And it will have been your doing.

CONTENTS

CONTENTS CONTINUED

INTRODUCTION

The power and ability available within every organisation has never ceased to amaze and excite me.

It is like the energy of an inexhaustible battery, waiting to be released and put to good use. In fact, it is eager to be used so.

People are the source.

When their power is released and directed, there always comes the first of many moments when a shiver goes down my spine, as I hear of the things that they have achieved of their own volition. It is always way beyond previous anticipation. There is no feeling like it.

After working with hundreds of organisations of every type over the last 55 years, I know that each organisation has had this capacity. Those with a top management team committed to realising that potential have always succeeded.

Success came when the top team truly grasped that their own individual actions were either the key to unlock the potential, or the lock which prevented its release.

Spending 25 years with the Toyota organisation took away previous misconceptions that some individuals had a 'special magic' to release this potential and replaced these false impressions with knowledge of a clear and repeatable method which anyone can apply, if they are personally committed to do so.

The method is not complicated. I wish I had a pound for each time a top executive said, "It can't be that simple!"

Its simplicity and, when explained, its feeling of common sense, is always an 'Aha!' moment.

Here I must caution that 'simple' should not be confused with 'easy,' and 'common sense' should not be confused with 'no need to do anything differently.'

This first book is written for members of top management, because we are the key to sustained and growing success. It explains how to unlock the potential of any organisation in a step-by-step and very practical way.

Expecting our organisation to reach its full potential without us personally taking the journey as leaders and pathfinders is a pipe dream, which many top management teams have learned the hard way.

If you are interested in the possibility of achieving previously unimagined progress in a sustained and continuously increasing way, could I ask you to take a very difficult first step?

Please put to one side the fact that, as top management, we are already very successful. Also, please be prepared to consider options which might be quite different to the methods, and especially the priorities, we have successfully employed thus far in our careers...

I had to do so after a 23-year successful career in General Motors, so I know, first-hand, how much effort this request requires. I also know the enormous personal and business benefits to be gained from doing so.

CHAPTER 1

AN UNUSUAL PLACE TO START

or

"Have we been focused on the right things?"

This concept was shown to three of us by a very senior member of the Toyota global leadership, back in 1992, during our first visit to Japan. As newly hired general managers, we all nodded and were quietly confident we understood this simple concept.

During the next 25 years with the company, it gradually became clear that this diagram is an amazing treasure. It underpins the whole of Toyota DNA and resolves much of the confusion people experience when trying to maximise the speed of an organisation's progress through employee engagement and good management.

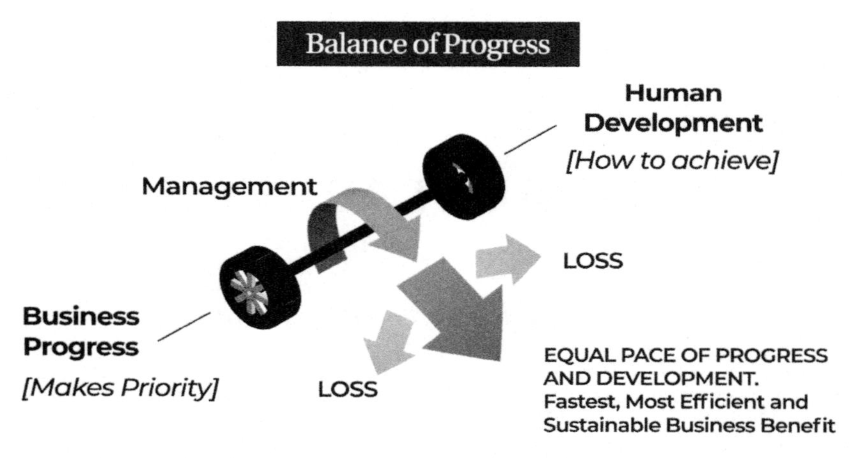

Putting it into words:

In every type of organisation there are two major elements which demand focus, the needs of the business itself and the development needs of the people employed in the business.

The two wheels are joined by a rigid axle. An imbalance of progress in either wheel results in loss of speed and direction and, therefore, potential business benefit.

This connection is the key to knowing how to continuously increase the power of the organisation whilst simultaneously accelerating the delivery of stakeholder objectives.

We, as members of top management, directly impact how this is reflected in our organisations.

In the following two sections, using the two extreme positions as comparators, is some explanation of why this is so.

FOCUS IS ONLY ON BUSINESS NEEDS

Focusing purely on business needs provides good short-term benefits. The management team work hard to improve performance and eliminate problems themselves. They tackle the issues which bring the big results.

Progress is rapid.

Soon the number of issues which give big payback reduce, and there is a need to tackle the smaller benefit problems. These items are no easier to resolve than the previous ones, they each demand just as much time and effort to resolve.

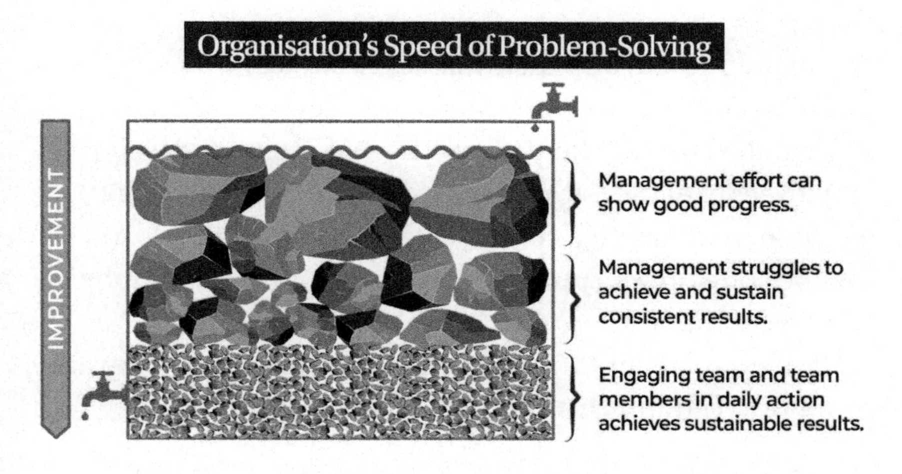

THE WATER LEVEL CAN BE LOWERED AS: demand fluctuates; lead-time reduces; process becomes faster; KAIZEN* increases

AS IT IS LOWERED PROBLEMS BECOME: more visible; more numerous

In this image the tank represents the organisation. The rocks represent problems which impede smooth progress and processing. The water level represents the resources and especially the level of inventory which has to be kept in place so that some continuity of processing can be maintained.

There just aren't enough capable heads, arms and legs available to resolve the number of issues needed to maintain the pace of progress.

The pace of business progress naturally reduces continuously, despite the best efforts of the management team.

Hiring external expertise to regain the pace increases costs. The solutions they provide struggle to sustain benefits.

After a time, the same problems start to come back again, because the people doing the job do not own the corrective actions taken.

FOCUS IS ONLY ON EMPLOYEE DEVELOPMENT

Top management, and their management team, see their role as delivering business results. In their eyes, it is the role of Human Resources, Training and Development to develop the employees. HRT&D are tasked with creating and delivering development training courses. Progress is measured by the number of courses, and places available, and the number of employees trained.

If the trainers or line managers are interviewed, they have common frustrations:

- "It is hard to fill the places on the courses, because the employees cannot be released from their important duties."
- "The employees come on the courses and rate them highly,

but somehow the training doesn't transfer back to the workplace. The employees come back to their jobs and carry on as before."

If the employees are interviewed they also have frustrations:

- "The course was great, but I was dragged away from the stuff I needed to do. I had to catch up when I got back."
- "Really good stuff, but not relevant to what I am struggling with right now on the job."

This is not to say that training courses deliver no value to the business. They unquestionably do and have big advantages in delivering consistent information.

The missing element is the direct connection between the development given and what specific development each individual employee needs right now to enable them to make the best business progress. This missing element makes it difficult to see the direct business benefit from this type of development. "What did we get for the money?"

The question to be considered is:

How to identify each employee's immediate needs in order to enable their maximum development and contribution to the benefit of the business?

ON THE JOB DEVELOPMENT LEARNING BY DOING

The ideal, balanced situation is that each employee receives the development they need, at the time they need it, to enable them to make the maximum contribution to benefit the business and to their own personal value.

This is naturally most practically identified by the employee themselves or their direct supervisor.

So, some questions spring to mind:

1. Do the supervisor and employee know that this is a vital part of their own responsibilities? Remember the two wheels? Does every level of management and supervision know that development of their people is 50% of their role?

2. How do the supervisor and employee go about identifying what are the most relevant development points to give the maximum business benefit in the current situation?

3. How does this requirement become an intrinsic part of the way business is done every day and at every level of the organisation?

The answers to these questions run through almost every part of this book.

To be clear, there is no conflict between the normally recognised formal training and OJD. Both are necessary in their correct application, as is technical or fundamental job skills training, which is often carried out on the job.

OJD is in addition to both of these. It is one of the key elements of maximising current and future benefits versus investment.

Using the tools and principles explained in the following chapters will answer these questions.

In the course of the book, some terms may be unfamiliar. Please don't worry, they will be explained, as they become relevant, later in the book.

CHAPTER 2

THE JOURNEY

or

Is the order of doing 'Good Stuff' important?

There are so many really good things available for any organisation to select:

- Books on management could fill whole libraries.
- Consultants offer an enormous variety of tools, philosophies, culture changes, psychological and motivational awareness.
- Study groups, institutes and fellowships abound.

Each of us has made good progress, both personally and professionally, using some or none of these combined, of course, with the added benefit of postgraduate studies at the 'school of hard knocks'.

But how do all these good things fit together, in an effective set, to get the best and most lasting results? How do we judge what should most effectively be used and in what sequence?

It became clear, after many years of working in Toyota, that there really is a set of very effective elements which, when implemented thoroughly and in the correct sequence, enables:

- Continually accelerating progress of the business.
- Continually accelerating development of the people.
- An excellent return for the time and money invested.
- Flexible and efficient response to changes in circumstances.

The sequence of effective use of these elements depends upon the 'maturity', or level of development, of the organisation.

Let me explain...

LEVELS OF MATURITY

There are surely many ways to measure the maturity of a company. This method is based upon the journey taken by Toyota, from the adventurous start in August 1937 to the current day. Multiple aspects of the journey could be shown: technological, cultural, financial, geographical and many others.

This analysis is of the organisation's management maturity. It is intended to allow any organisation to benchmark their current level on the ladder of maturity.

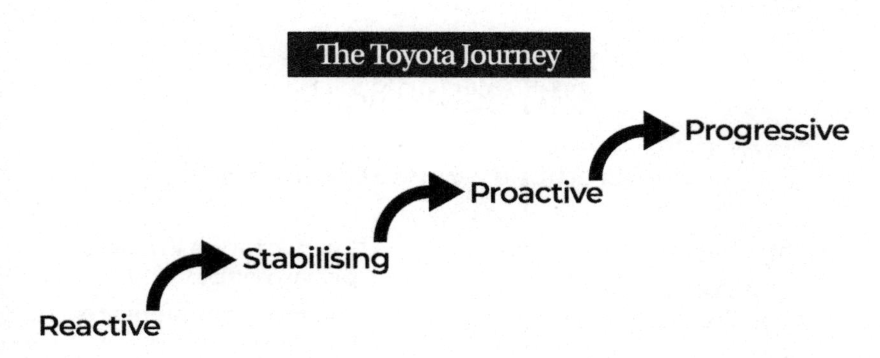

It can be successfully applied to any organisation which provides products and/or services to customers. It introduces the important order of progress which is essential to real, sustained and continuously improving success.

In the following pages, the characteristics visible at each level of maturity are explained. The levels or stages are generic and can be applied to all types of organisation and at many organisational levels.

Life is not simple, so different parts of any business will be at different levels and even one part will have elements across many levels. However, so far, each business which has assessed itself against the levels has been able to decide at which stage their business is currently operating.

REACTIVE

The first level of maturity, 'Reactive,' often begins where an organisation has grown beyond the point where simple, daily contact is enough to manage the business effectively. The boss doesn't have time to deal personally with every issue or decision, and the assumption that 'everybody knows what to do' is no longer true. Very large and even multinational businesses have found themselves in this situation, although it is not always recognised internally.

Reactive

Low Credibility with Stakeholders

- Struggle to meet targets
- Little teamwork between departments
- Management under constant pressure
- Survive from day to day
- Maintenance considered an expense
- People considered an expense
- Every change impacts performance
- Too many problems to handle
- Too complex to prioritise
- The loudest voice wins
- Customer satisfaction low
- Employee satisfaction low

Management struggle alone
Do top management recognise reality?

The symptoms the organisation experiences are shown in the diagram. Typical statements from the leader of a Reactive organisation are:

- "The management board is just not acting as a team."
- "We cannot seem to connect with our people."
- "This business is much more complex than others, it is not as simple as making cars."

There often comes a point at which the pressure on the leader, or one of the board members, makes external support to change the culture an attractive option.

The image of 'Lean' (when interpreted as efficiency improvement) is often seen, and even recommended, as the correct way forward. Lean, in terms of headcount or inventory reduction, will provide temporary business KPI (key performance indicator) improvements, but will be unsustainable at this stage. Lean will get a bad name. "It is just making things harder and harder."

STABILISING

It is always necessary to move from 'Reactive' to 'Stabilising' before challenging what Toyota would recognise as kaizen, or 'improvements which are above the current standard.'

The Stabilising level provides the foundation upon which new progress can be built. Without it, the improvements sink as if they were built on quicksand.

Stabilising

Performance and credibility improve

- Total work process flow visible
- Teamwork improving
- Priority by best total business result
- Decisions based upon facts
- Customer quality is built-in
- Direction becomes clear to all
- People able to contribute more and more
- Problems solved permanently
- KPI improvements remain
- Maintenance becoming a priority
- Change still disturbs performance

Employee engagement and contribution grows

It is not unusual to see evidence of what has become known as 'Lean Tool' implementation in organisations at the Reactive or Stabilising levels. For example, evidence of process balancing, cell processing or single item flow, inventory management and 4S (5S) can be seen. All of these items are specific tools and will be explained in detail later in the book.

The tools are there in appearance but do not provide the benefits of which they are capable. Their benefits are negated by the high levels of losses within and between the processes, many of which are a direct result of the overburdening which the 'Lean Tools' apply when used at these levels.

Examples of these losses are: customer quality and delivery problems, the need for in-house reprocessing because of work errors, process delays because of machine or system failure and delays because of missing or late materials or information.

Many of the elements needed to move from Reactive to Stabilising fall under the scope of the 'Toyota Way.' This was published within the corporation 20 years ago to enable new ventures, especially outside Japan, to understand the background or foundation needed for continuous improvement (kaizen) to succeed and sustain.

Moving from the Reactive to the Stabilising level provides very substantial business benefits as progress is made.

PROACTIVE

At the 'Proactive' level of maturity, the application of structured and targeted kaizen adds value, and continuous improvements in standards and expectations will be achieved.

(In the context of this book, kaizen refers to the use of the Toyota Production System. Please do not be put off by the term 'production system,' by the way. TPS is applicable to every type of organisation which delivers a service or product.)

Proactive

Stakeholders see a well-managed organisation

- Targets regularly achieved
- One team
- Big problem solving capacity at the shop floor
- Seven wastes reducing
- Fewer and fewer problems
- Planned maintenance done religiously
- People are more and more professional
- Changes anticipated and managed
- Customer is king
- Good analysis of facts drives direction
- Future vision and plans clear to all

Performance breaking new boundaries

Engagement of the workforce in achieving business objectives becomes increasingly effective.

There are also increasing opportunities to delegate whole missions to the workforce with confidence that the assignments will be handled effectively, efficiently and within the policies of the organisation.

The workforce is continuously increasing in ability and professionalism.

Consequently, management have enough time to thoroughly consider the future and lead the organisation to be ready, in advance, for upcoming changes of circumstances or for potential opportunities.

The business becomes able to manage changes quickly and with minimum disruption to performance (flexibility).

PROGRESSIVE

Through the 'Progressive' level, the organisation becomes increasingly powerful in the ability to deliver continuously better business results and to handle changes.

Progressive

Stakeholders trust management direction

- Challenge targets regularly achieved
- Everyone involved in achieving Vision
- TPM in place and costs reducing safely
- People are professionals
- Processes learn from experience
- Problem-solving skills used to make plans
- Performance step-change done regularly
- Capacity increasing at no extra cost
- New business opportunities can be sought

Flexibility and additional capacity created

Targets are set and achieved which truly challenge the business to reach previously unimaginable performance. Zero accidents, zero defects, zero losses during changes or kaizen implementation are typical targets for an organisation at this level of maturity. These are meaningful objectives, because the whole workforce will analyse the current conditions within their responsibility, identify the issues and opportunities, make concrete plans to achieve them and deliver on time.

Under these circumstance the business can move from "What can I do to satisfy my customers better and get new business?" to "What is the role of my company in society, now and in the future?".

Toyota in Japan has been at this level for 20 years or more. The groundbreaking innovations of hybrid technology and hydrogen fuel cell technology to meet climate change are well known.

Many people are surprised to hear that the company also has an established housebuilding business which uses all of the 'Lean Tools.' The houses are module manufactured off-site and installed in a few days whilst maintaining, or exceeding, expected durability, comfort, individuality and attractiveness, with class-leading environmental and technological performance.

The company also foresaw the impact of a rapidly ageing population profile and increased longevity. For more than 20 years, the company has been steadily developing affordable, domestic robot support for infirm and elderly people.

SELF-EVALUATION

Most of us work in established organisations. Some of us are fortunate enough to experience the tremendous satisfaction of starting a new venture from scratch, but relatively few.

Once the organisation is established, our role is generally

to improve upon what already exists. As we see from the four levels of maturity, there is enormous scope and potential.

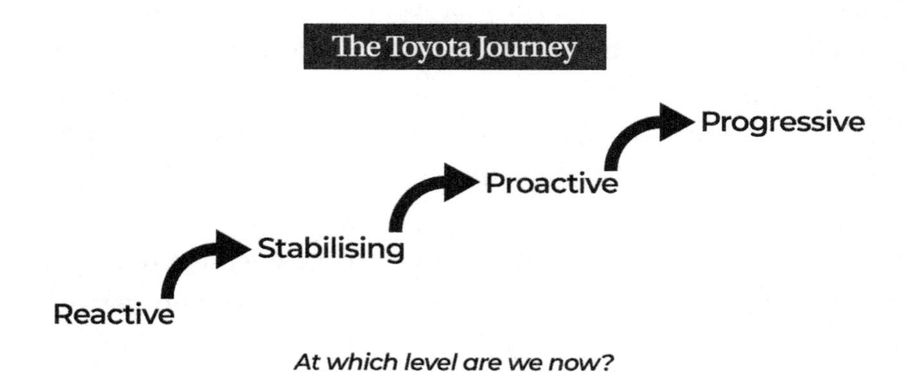

At which level are we now?

Step 1 is to grasp where our organisation is on the journey to maturity.

Factual assessment is critical in everything we do from now on. Remember the golden rules of self-evaluation.

If we say "we already do this", we have to answer the questions:

1. What percentage of the organisation actually does this as normal business?
2. In the places where it is done, how effective is it in achieving business benefit?

Then we can judge more accurately where we are.

Reactive (Level 1) is not uncommon. Organisations of all sizes and types can be at this level. The management team recognise many of the issues but often attribute this to the fact that "Our business is different, it is not so simple". This is an entirely natural view in these circumstances.

SECTION ONE
FROM REACTIVE TO STABILISING

We do want to get the business benefits from increased maturity, but we don't make cars and we are not Toyota, in fact we are not even manufacturers.

"SO HOW DO WE GO ABOUT IT?"

CHAPTERS 3 TO 11 COVER THE STEPS TOWARDS STABILISING MATURITY LEVEL

CHAPTER 3

GETTING STARTED

STEP 1 FROM REACTIVE TO STABILISING

The move from Reactive to Stabilising is a major change. It brings many concrete business benefits in terms of safety, customer satisfaction, quality, delivery on time and, as a result, costs.

It is achieved through **harnessing the engagement of the whole organisation**.

Reactive to Stabilising

REACTIVE		STABILISING
Low credibility with stakeholders		Performance and credibility improve
• Struggle to meet targets • Little teamwork between departments • Management under constant pressure • Survive from day today • Maintenance considered an expense • People considered an expense • Every change impact performance • Too many problems to handle • Too complex to prioritise • The loudest voice wins • Customer satisfaction low • Employee satisfaction low		• Total process flow visible • Teamwork improving • Priority by best total business result • Decisions based upon the facts • Customer quality is built-in • Direction becomes clear to all • People able to contribute more • Problem is solved permanently • KPI improvements remain • Maintenance becoming a priority • Change still disturbs performance
Management struggle alone		Employee engagement and contribution grows

There are two key points to remember:

1. The changes are rooted in the behaviour and priorities of the top executive and his or her team. Success or failure sits firmly with us.
2. It is also important that we remember that this first step of stabilising is how we lay the foundation for the next two levels, Proactive and Progressive.

Skipping or short-cutting the Stabilising stage will prevent other progress being permanent and sustainable.

There are many examples of organisations which have tried to implement employee engagement successfully. There are also many, even among global and national organisations, which have found themselves wondering what they have achieved with their efforts and investment.

There is a pattern which can be seen again and again:

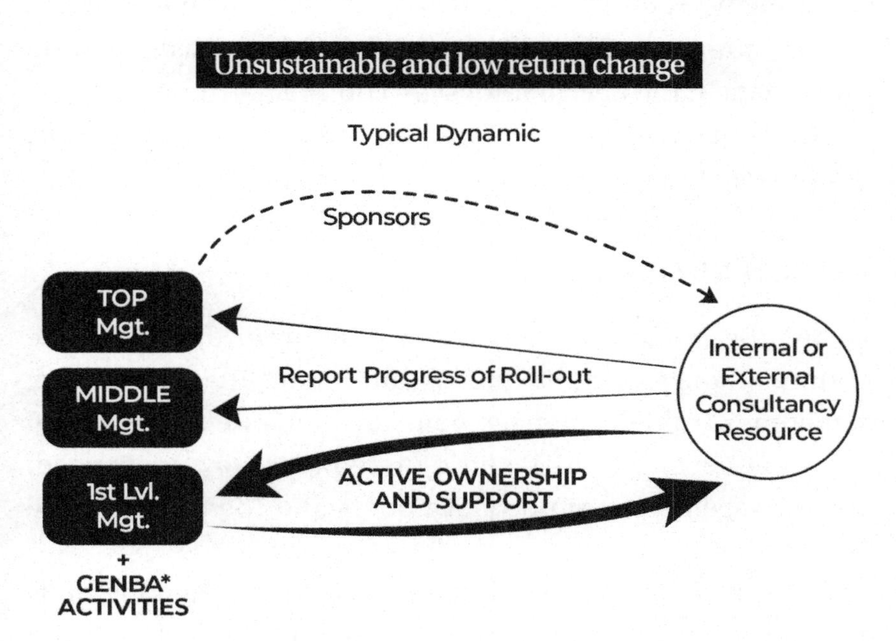

The company engages an internal or external body to implement elements of engagement, such as visual management boards, daily team meetings and even more direct elements of the Toyota Production System, such as process balancing and single item flow.

The implementation is done at department, section or team level by the internal or external consultants and this engagement makes progress for 3 to 10 years. During that time, I know of many organisations which have spent between £30m and £40m directly on these activities.

In each case, towards the end of the implementation period, the organisations have asked themselves what business benefit is actually coming from the investment and these activities. The improvement in the bottom line generally does not reflect the investment and effort expended.

In the interim period, top management receive very encouraging reports of progress. Each month, the progress in the number of people/teams/departments which have implemented the new methods are continually improving.

There are two main reasons for the lack of measurable, bottom line business benefits.

REASON NUMBER ONE

Firstly, the implementation is not done from the top to the bottom management of the organisation. The upper and, sometimes, middle management are not directly involved. Their methods, priorities and requirements stay unchanged. The management team do not understand their roles in the new methods.

In these circumstances, the employees like the new methods but recognise that they have to operate in parallel with the original way of doing things, especially where management is involved.

The new methods sustain in a very limited form and are not directly connected to the business priorities.

Without exception, every successful, sustained and continually improving implementation of 'Lean' has started from the very top of the organisation and been cascaded down through the management line.

(Please make no mistake, the organisation follows what the top management do, *not what they say. Employees watch closely where and when the top management fully engage and know that these are the true priorities and the true policies. They judge engagement by where top management chooses to spend their time and which items they choose to support in a practical way, by doing something themselves.*

> In a nutshell, as top management, be sure to put your body where your priorities are.

Employees are bombarded with exhortations on a daily basis: "Safety First", "The Customer is King", "Quality is Number One". Slogan after slogan, poster after poster which never translates into physical and practical follow-up or coaching by top management. Employees quickly develop immunity to them. They need to do so because their reality does not gel with the slogans.)

Guaranteed success comes when the very top of the organisation engage with experienced practitioners to learn for themselves by actually doing. This needs to be combined with the recognition (illustrated in the two-wheel, Balance of Progress diagram at the start of this book) that their role is to use every business priority to coach their people during the actual job (i.e. On the Job Development).

The real difficulties top management initially struggle with in physically doing these two things will be explored in more detail later in the book. The practical methods of overcoming them will also be explained.

REASON NUMBER TWO

Secondly, the methods and tools are learned or taught in an incomplete way and small, but vital, key points are missed. Although small, these elements often make the difference between delivering real business benefit or not. Mainly this derives from the advisors having worked in a 'Lean' organisation, and understanding what they did very well, but not having had the opportunity to see the bigger picture or the underlying structures and connections.

A very common example of this is the implementation of status visualisation, i.e. continuously displaying the current situation for everyone to see, usually on whiteboards, and team meetings to review the boards and respond. The boards are made and the meetings start. The engagement of the team increases immediately. The small details of which type of visualisation – tables, graphs, pie charts, etc. – and how to connect the displayed items to the company priorities are almost always missed. These details make a dramatic difference in the business benefit and employee development and engagement gained from the effort.

It is also not uncommon for the advisors to know the tools they have used and bring them to the organisation as a fait accompli, indicating "this is the way it must be done".

Most organisations already have tools which are well established through many years of application. Throwing away the current tools and bringing in new ones in their place creates a resistance which is hard to overcome. The tools which fulfil previously unaddressed requirements are much more easily assimilated.

Wherever possible, the terms used in this book refer to the purpose of each activity and avoid unnecessarily specifying particular tools. Using, or modifying, the tools with which an organisation is already comfortable makes much more effective and efficient progress.

OK... I am the chief exec. This is my top team. So, what should we be doing that we aren't already?

The following activities are to enable the top team to learn, by doing it themselves first, the things that they will expect from their people going forward. This is vital, enabling the top team to set their expectations very clearly and, as importantly, to coach their own teams as part of daily business as usual.

The activities themselves must be done by the top team, but the administration and arrangements to allow this to happen can take too much time.

Most chief execs have a corporate or administration section, or both, to support them. One of these sections could be tasked with supporting the top team in the background. Many diary adjustments, invitations, practical resource preparation, etc. will be required.

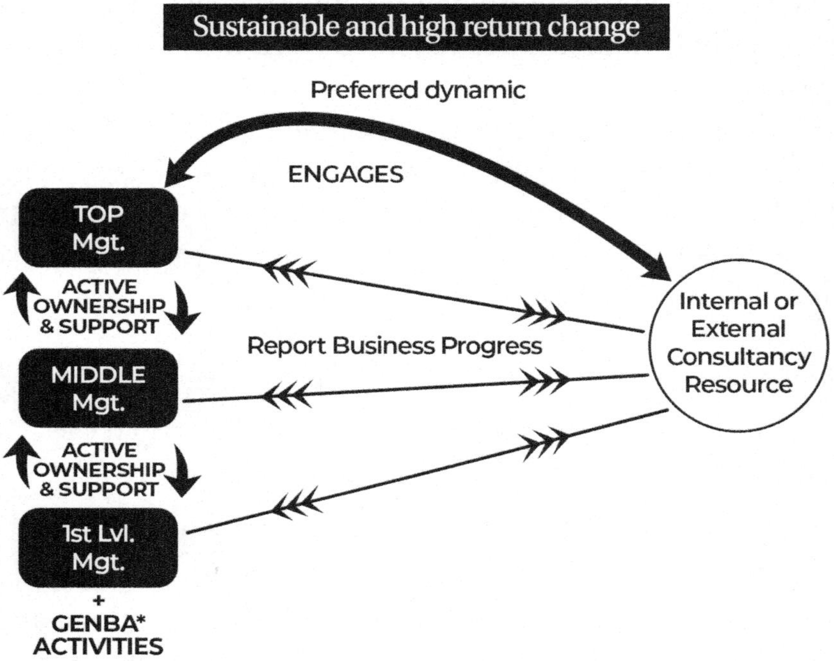

Sustainable and high return change

Preferred dynamic

ENGAGES

TOP Mgt.

ACTIVE OWNERSHIP & SUPPORT

Report Business Progress

Internal or External Consultancy Resource

MIDDLE Mgt.

ACTIVE OWNERSHIP & SUPPORT

1st Lvl. Mgt.

+

GENBA* ACTIVITIES

The creation of the system (i.e. what is needed and where it belongs) is the top team's responsibility and should not be delegated. Naturally, the chief exec has the final decision in this area.

The admin support can do the actual modifications and, after the system has become useful and effective, can make it pretty for sharing with others outside the top team.

Most organisations modify their work many times during the first few weeks, and even months, as their understanding and experience grows. This is a good thing.

In answering the question "What are the requirements for employees to be able to contribute most effectively and enjoy their work?" there are four main elements that management need to ensure are in place and effective.

Basic Requirements for Employee Engagement

›››**UNDERSTAND SITUATION CORRECTLY**
- True data
- Company direction

›››**ABLE TO IMPACT (MAIN MOTIVATOR)**
- Time
- Problem solving skills (Root cause countermeasure)
- Management support
- Technical skills (job specific)

›››**ABLE TO PRIORITISE**
- Clear guidelines
- Pareto and severity analysis

›››**ADDITIONAL MOTIVATION**
- Visualisation
- Management involvement
- Management recognition
- The ANDON*

THE COMPLETE SET IS NECESSARY FOR BEST AND SUSTAINED RESULTS

They are for the employee:

1. **To be able to understand the situation correctly**.
2. To be **able to impact** the situation through their efforts. (This is the main motivator for everyone in the workplace.)
3. To be **able to** correctly **prioritise** their actions.
4. To receive **additional motivation** from their leader(s).

1. **Understanding the situation correctly** requires the availability and use of true data which simply, and accurately, reflects the business status. (So many companies are now expanding the use of such data-gathering tools as SAP software. These provide a very useful source for the first level of analysis, but they are not a prerequisite.)

It also requires clarity from the company and their leader regarding the direction in which they are expected to go. This is best provided by an annual policy deployment activity, which systematically involves and engages all levels of the organisation deciding where to go and how to get there. In Toyota, it is the Hoshin Kanri process. In this book, I have called it Direction Deployment to make the activity more easily understood.

2. **Being able to impact the business progress** of the company requires, of course, time to work on the important issues, especially to do sufficient analysis to ensure effective actions are taken. This means paid time which is clearly allocated for this purpose.

   Problem-solving skills, which enable the employees to find the true root cause of the problems they are experiencing and to be able to permanently eliminate them, are essential. This is the single most neglected element and the most important for sustained progress. Support enables the difficulties employees experience in their improvement activities to be quickly overcome.

   Finally, of course, they need the necessary technical or job specific skills.

3. **The ability for employees to confidently prioritise** their actions requires clear guidelines from the company upon which they can safely depend. ("If I follow this sequence of priorities the company will always support my actions, even if they are not the most expedient on this occasion.")

   In some companies a simple hierarchy of priorities is provided, for example:

1. Safety
2. Customer satisfaction
3. Quality
4. Correct output volume
5. Efficiency
6. Cost

So, if I have a safety issue and a customer satisfaction issue at the same time, I know the company will expect me to handle the safety issue first.

When a problem has been investigated, there are usually several facets which need to be addressed.

To prioritise these Pareto analysis is very clear and useful. This simple tool is dramatically undervalued, or even missing, in the majority of problem-solving methods used.

Of course, if any issue is in the category of "Fix it now or we will suffer big damage" it is naturally top priority.

4. **Additional motivation** comes from visualisation of the whole situation and the results of actions taken.

   Management involvement is demonstrated by being on the spot and offering positive and practical support which allows employees to truly challenge their capability in a safe and highly effective environment.

   Recognition is best given for specific actions and public appreciation at the regular meetings or specially arranged recognition meetings. The boss saying, "Wow! That analysis was clearly tough to do but gave us so much clarity, thank you for that!" is the type of recognition meant. Simply saying a general "well done" is better than nothing but not a very strong motivator.

FOUR TOOLS OF EMPLOYEE ENGAGEMENT

The four requirements and their sub-elements are incorporated in the following four management tools. Applying these in the correct order and with thoroughness will deliver high and effective employee engagement and priority business results.

1. **Visualisation and the use of facts**
2. **Go and See (See Chapter 5)**
3. **Practical Problem-Solving**
4. **Direction Deployment**

Interwoven with these are many other sub-elements which will be explained as we go.

The tools are a set. The use of one or more of them will bring benefits, but only the full set will change the culture and power of an organisation to move from Reactive to Stabilising and from there to Proactive.

IMPLEMENTATION ORDER

The tools are listed in the order of implementation which will create a natural 'pull' for the subsequent elements in turn.

Creating a 'pull' situation, where the people involved can feel the need for the next element, is very helpful for all concerned. It transforms "do it because I say so" into "we can see the need to do this".

There is also a 'Rule of Twelve' at play here. The power of the tools are not visible to everyone at the concept, understanding stage. Only actually doing and seeing the results brings full appreciation. Therefore, please use the tools twelve times, even if you are uncertain in the beginning. I promise that, long before the twelfth application of the tools, their importance to achieving ever improving performance will become very clear. The tools will become your own.

Although the order of implementation makes a big difference to the ease of introduction, the importance of each element cannot be overstated. Learning the full set by doing them repeatedly will change the culture of the organisation in a very positive way. Top management will find that they are prioritising their time differently than before and achieving much better business results by doing so.

CHAPTER 4

VISUALISATION

ENGAGEMENT TOOL 1
VISUALISATION AND THE USE OF FACTS

ENGAGEMENT TOOL 1A

CREATING VISUALISATION

The start point is visualisation of the current situation based upon facts and data.

Being the first element to be implemented, the purpose and benefits may not be immediately understood by the participants and so can require some persuasion to make happen. The head of the organisation needs to lead from the front.

Making the first visualisation of the current situation is a very practical step.

I would ask you just to do the activities and we can talk about the underlying psychological, sociological and management principles later on, but please remember, the first principle for this, as for the implementation of every element, is for everyone to learn by doing these things themselves, starting with the top team, as a team.

Firstly, gather the top team together and visualise on a wall or whiteboard how the business operates, starting from delivery to the customer, back through each stage of the process to the setting of the schedule and/or plan. At each stage of the visualised process, show the key performance indicators which are used to decide the performance level of that stage.

It doesn't have to be perfect, and it doesn't have to be neat. Just make a quick start.

(I usually start with a pile of blank, A4 sheets of paper, Blu Tack and a marker pen. By just making the shape of the visualisation, with each element represented by an A4 sheet, with the title of the division, department, KPI, etc., it is possible to involve the whole team in the process.)

It does have to start from delivery of the product or service to the customer and work back, step by step, from there. The KPIs of safety, quality to the customer, delivery on time, and cost are the minimum required.

An appropriate timescale should be decided: daily, weekly or monthly measurements. Daily is best to start with, to make fast progress and learning, then weekly and monthly visualisation can follow. (Some service organisations can only start with weekly.)

Secondly, decide which of the top team is the owner of the results of each process and make the visualisation clearly delineated by that ownership. (Put the name, not the department on the picture.)

Thirdly, each owner should confirm the target of each of their KPIs and arrange for the daily, etc., result to be collected and updated on their KPIs.

At this stage, there will be many discussions and probably many changes, so keep it simple to move elements around and remove, add or change things.

Daily meetings usually utilise simple, daily results versus the planned result or the target for the day. One number versus another.

The visualisation should have a place for the team to write their agreed priorities and also a pace to list the agreed actions, the owner of each action and the date at which the owner will report back to the meeting.

The making of the visualisation will begin the process of team making and also make responsibilities crystal clear.

ENGAGEMENT TOOL 1B

USING THE VISUALISATION

MEETING STRUCTURE

The top team will need to meet frequently to make the visualisation. Daily, at a fixed time, is the best. Ad hoc meetings are not very effective and convey the wrong priorities.

The first draft visualisation should take only 2 or 3 days to create.

A fixed, 45-minute slot in the day, at which the top team will meet, is best. The meeting itself will quickly become 30 minutes or even less. The 45 minutes will allow time for any discussions and arrangements between attendees to happen immediately after the meeting.

From the first draft creation, the visualisation becomes a tool for the top team to grasp the condition of the processes. It should be on a daily basis.

It must be a standing meeting. This is a strict rule. The benefits will quickly become obvious.

The chair of the meeting is the chief executive.

Starting from the customer results first, and then working back, each owner in turn states their results and their actions regarding any issues that become visible.

At this meeting, it is only necessary for what will be done by when to be explained. The actions can be noted as a follow-up item at the next, or a subsequent, meeting if the chief exec thinks it helpful.

The purposes of the daily meeting will become clear just by doing them, but here are some of the most important:

1. The top team can see the total performance picture and will know which areas of the business need special attention.

The parts of the business which are the bottlenecks will become visible. By focusing upon those, the top team can make rapid progress in increasing the output/efficiency of the whole business with the minimum time and effort.

2. The whole visualisation is made from the customer's requirements and then working backwards from there. This will automatically place the priority of every process in the business upon the outcome for the customer. Many previously invisible or unsolvable differences in priorities between departments and divisions will be resolved.

3. The issues which require teamwork between divisions will become clear and can be followed up.

The meeting will soon eliminate much of the agendas of other meetings, so the meeting time will not be additional diary time. In fact, the meetings will liberate more diary time.

ENGAGEMENT TOOL 1C

CASCADE OF VISUALISATION

Once the top team are confidently realising the benefits of the daily meeting, it is good to begin the roll-out of such meetings to their subordinates and, finally, to the hands-on teams.

Some of the key points for this are:

1. Ensure that the KPI targets, at each level of the organisation, add up to the target level to which they report.

2. Allow the teams to make their own visualisation and to learn by doing so. As long as the basic KPIs are present, there is no need for the visualisations of each team to have the same content. Each team will have unique issues to follow.

3. Keep the meeting disciplines at each level.

BEGIN WITH A LIMITED MODEL AREA FOR EACH STAGE

The top team's activity is the first model. But it is wise to choose a model area for each subsequent stage and activity. Why?

- The introduction of each new element will have many learning points which can only be discovered through actually doing it. Several cycles of try, learn and modify will undoubtedly be needed.
- The ability to modify quickly and try again is very valuable. It allows the fastest progress and the best outcome, which can then be shared with others.
- Once a large-scale roll-out has begun, it is very cumbersome to modify and fine tune the methods used. Important details, which make a large difference to the business benefits and development of the employees, are too often compromised because of this.

REMEMBER THE TWO WHEELS OF BEST PROGRESS!

When choosing a model area, or the sequence of roll-out, always prioritise by which will best meet the current business priorities. The implementation of the elements of employee engagement are not academic exercises! Each activity should provide business benefits in line with the business priorities at the fastest pace.

By aligning the activity and the business priorities, there is never a conflict in the minds of the people involved about whether they have time to do as requested. In essence, these methods become "The way we do things around here".

The implementation of each step should always bring business benefits in the most needed area.

MEETING TONE AND CULTURE

The tone and culture of the meetings should be agreed by all participants. This is very important for effectiveness.

Some strongly recommended ground rules/disciplines are:

1. Discussion is based upon facts only, no opinion, no historical examples. Go and see the actual situation before reporting or commenting.
2. No criticism, even in 'jest'; we are all doing our best.
3. If there is a better idea, please share it at the time of the discussion. If not, please follow the idea, upon which consensus is reached, as if it were your own.
4. If another division is thought to be the cause of an issue, please ensure that you tell them in time for them to be prepared to answer at the meeting.
5. If an owner is not available for the meeting, it is their responsibility to ensure someone attends in their place and has full authority to make decisions and commitments.
6. All agreed follow-up actions must have an owner and a firm report-back date.
7. Potential risks to performance should be shared with the team as soon as they are identified.
8. The whole team succeeds or fails together. Not asking for or offering help, when needed, is a major problem.

Following such ground rules may require a little time for some of the top team to make it their 'natural' style. The chief executive may need to be firm in ensuring they are followed strictly to help them change long-established, and even previously rewarded, habits.

Occasionally, the rest of the team may have to remind the chief executive.

The benefits of adhering to such pre-agreed disciplines cannot be overemphasised.

It is important to remember that this meeting is not to duplicate or replace the role of each of the owners. The meeting is to look at the *total performance* of the organisation from the stakeholder's perspective, especially the customers, and to prioritise accordingly.

Weekly and monthly meetings usually utilise trend graphs. It may be helpful for the top team to accept some training in how to interpret this format. The target is that the graphs tell a story and not just a result.

Later sections of the book may be helpful:

- The most helpful graph format.
- How to visualise results judgements.

The implementation of the appropriate visualisation at each level of the organisation and daily, weekly and monthly follow-up standing meetings will address the foundation requirements for employee engagement.

These meetings will quickly replace much, if not all, of the value-added contents of other current meetings and, as a result, will become more effective and efficient.

At the working team level, the frequency of follow-up changes from daily to hourly.

Results come from what happens hour by hour in the

workplace. Immediate understanding and reaction is critical. True facts are available to be grasped, enabling effectiveness and speed of problem resolution.

PRODUCTION CONTROL BOARDS

The use of, what Toyota would call, Production Control Boards is very helpful. Each hour's actual quality output versus the plan is noted, as is the cumulative result hour by hour. Also, the cause of any loss versus the plan is written down by the team leader or a designated team member. Each single minute of loss should be accounted for. This information provides the basis for both immediate actions and subsequent problem elimination.

A word of caution here. It is natural that once such data gathering is made, the next urge is to try to automate the collection of the information. It is seen as 'efficiency improvement.' The automation consumes many hours of very skilled specialist time during which nothing changes except the quality of the information collected, both for the better and worse.

Much more value is added for the people, working in the area, to begin grasping the information in real time and start trying to permanently eliminate the losses, prioritised by their impact, to the business result. The specialist and engineer time is better spent supporting this activity. This directly impacts the bottom line. Data, by itself, is not of value. **Using** the data is where the value is added.

This is not a paper-based versus paperless management argument. However, I recommend starting simply with paper first and move to software only where it is truly beneficial and maintains real-time human involvement.

EXAMPLES OF VISUALISATION

DAILY RESULTS FOR TOTAL ORGANISATION

The visualisation was initially made by the top team using blank, A5 sheets with the subject handwritten in felt tip. The top set of photos shows the total processes visualised, as a second draft version, with proposed KPIs identified and their owners specified.

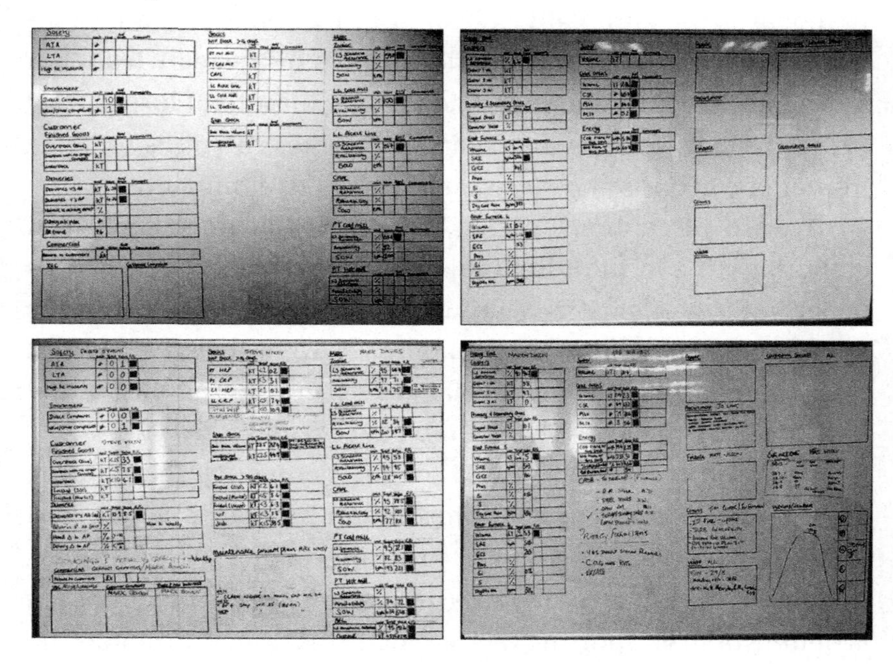

The lower set of pictures shows the targets for each KPI decided and the daily results being entered on to the boards.

The top team met, for 20 minutes at 12:15, every day to review the results and to reach consensus about the priorities of the issues from a total operation's perspective. This ensured that the resources were allocated to the issues which would provide the best total business benefit. Weekly and monthly boards followed quickly. For speed of grasping the situation, red highlights indicated a KPI not reaching the daily target.

For daily visualisation boards a simple comparison of planned result versus actual is fine.

EXAMPLES OF VISUALISATION

MONTHLY RESULTS FOR TOTAL ORGANISATION

At the monthly level, the KPIs are visualised as trends. The method of graphing is consistent throughout, depending upon whether it is a simple KPI result or a summary of progress versus activity plans.

The consistent method is very important for maximising information whilst maintaining simplicity and speed of grasping the situation.

The top team met at 13:00 on the second Thursday of the month for an hour. This consisted of:

- 20 minutes to grasp the results.
- 10 minutes for feedback on follow-up actions.
- 15 minutes for explanations of Practical Problem-Solving actions and progress.
- 15 minutes for separate discussions to arrange joint Go and See exercises for issues raised.
- The head of the organisation coaches his team during the meetings.

In this organisation, the visualisation follows the organisation's structure, rather than process flow, but it was still very effective in setting priorities and making cross-functional correlations. The visualisation quickly led to the organisation identifying and realising many tens of millions of GBP savings and cost avoidance through problem-solving and kaizen.

VISUALISATION GRAPHS

THE KEY POINTS

Top management has no time to stand and study a myriad of graphic styles to try to grasp the key issues. During meetings and Go and See exercises, there will be many graphic representations to take in.

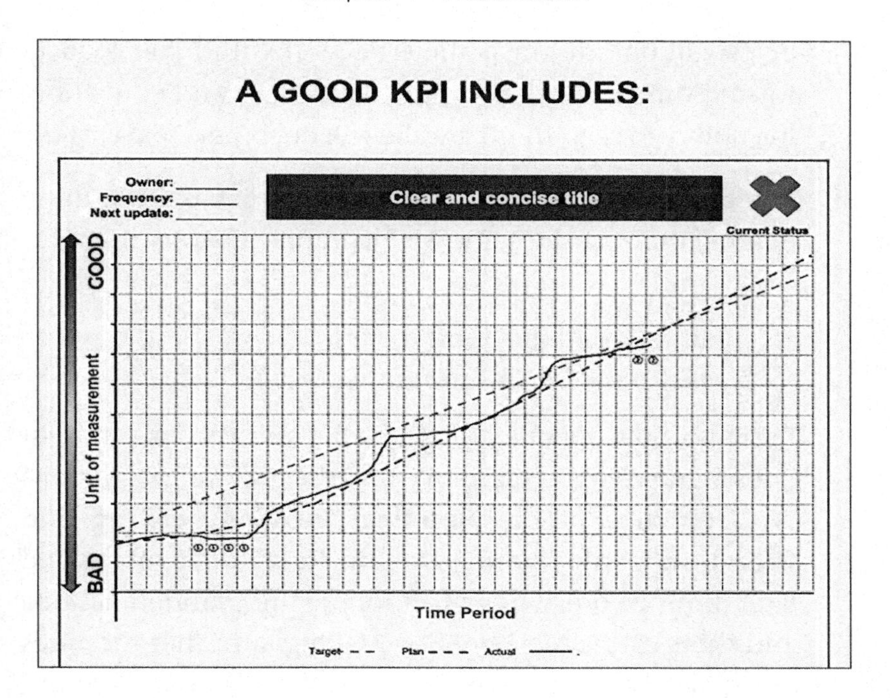

At the monthly meeting, there may be 40-50 graphs on the wall. Which ones should the meeting spend time discussing? When we focus on one graph, what information is most helpful to decide what kind of follow-up is most appropriate?

There is a **90 second rule** for all visualisations which says that anyone looking at the displayed data should be able to grasp the total status and which areas to focus in on within 90 seconds of starting to look.

Therefore, a standard format with standard signals is very helpful for all concerned.

1. A trend graph tells the maximum information with the minimum effort. The ability to grasp the history of progress and judge if the situation is chronic, one-off, consistent or varying really helps conversations. Simply OK or NG (no good) for this one period results in wasted time in initial

investigations to grasp the true status and can lead to wasted time and effort overall. With time and education, the ability to read trend graphs will become a real asset.

2. Three lines are needed and their format is important. Again if they are the same for all graphs it is very helpful:

   - A red dotted line for the target.
   - A black dotted line for the plan.
   - A black solid line for the actual result.

   Initially, most organisations are able only to make straight lines for targets and plans because the planning is shallow. With practice of the **Practical Problem-Solving** and **Direction Deployment / Hoshin Kanri** tools, explained later, both of these lines will follow the planned actions and their estimated benefits. Making sure that the lines are in place from the beginning enables discussions about the level of planning in place.

3. Some graphs show a positive outcome if the result line goes up, for example profits, whilst others show a positive outcome when going down, for example costs. It is very helpful to put a simple standard arrow showing which is a positive direction for this graph.

4. The name of the owner of the KPI should be prominently shown. Please ensure that this is a person's name, not a department or section name. The owner is the person responsible for delivering the target and for reporting progress versus plan. Very often many people have to work to improve one KPI, but the owner is still responsible for the delivery of the total result and the judgement of that result.

5. The judgement of the result for the period should be shown in a consistent position on all graphs. Habitually,

I have used the top right-hand corner. The judgement symbol should be clearly visible from 3 metres minimum and in the following standard format:

Progress is in line with, or better than plan. No need to focus on this item.

Progress is less than plan, but the owner can recover without additional support.

Progress is less than plan. Owner is '**pulling the Andon**'* for support.

**See Chapter 10 for an explanation of Andon.*

The standards for the graphic visualisations are very detailed and specific. They may seem even pedantic at first. They have been developed over generations of practice and have proven themselves to be the most effective and efficient method.

Following them from day one, even without grasping the full implications and benefits of these methods versus others, will pay huge benefits in the speed of progress and in the usefulness of the tools.

The insistence upon keeping the standards will only be effective if it comes from the very top of the organisation. This often means immediate reaction when the standard is not followed.

CHAPTER 5

GO AND SEE

ENGAGEMENT TOOL 2
GO & SEE

The next step in the order is Go & See.

If your first reaction is "I keep seeing this stuff about 'Go and See for myself' in books, but it is impossible for me to do, as I am too busy as it is! Besides, that is what I pay my people for!" I would ask for your patience for a while. (I also said the same thing loudly and often in the beginning.)

For the time being, please consider that some of the things upon which we spend our time and focus may not be the optimum things which consistently and sustainedly improve the performance of the business. This is the most fundamental thing being a Toyota executive taught me. (*I used to joke with my colleagues that moving to the Toyota way was easy; all I had to do was take my head off and put it back on facing the other way!*) The things I used to focus upon were actually only the results. I learned to spend my time and energy on improving the process, which delivered more and better results.

This is really two topics, by the way.

Go, See and Understand.
&
Go, Support and Coach

They are together because they happen at the same time.

However, it may be useful to explain them one by one.

ENGAGEMENT TOOL 2A
GO, SEE & UNDERSTAND

Why is Go, See & Understand so important?

- It saves your time. (Counter-intuitive, but fact.)
- It saves your people's time. (Counter-intuitive, but fact.)
- It ensures a culture of facts only.
- It ensures problems are resolved in the shortest time.

For companies in the transition towards Stabilising the most important 'Go and See' is to grasp the actual condition of urgent or priority issues.

You and your people simply do not have time to go and see everything. How will your people know when to call you?

ESCALATION RULES

To support this, companies usually make a set of escalation rules. Often they are in a simple table form. This is a very basic example.

ISSUE	TO SUPERVISOR	TO MANAGER	TO DIRECTOR
Safety incident	Needs company occ. health visit	Needs external treatment	Will result in lost time for injured person.
Quality defect	Can correct immediately	Leaks to next department	Leaks to customer
Volume loss	Less than 30 minutes	More than 30 minutes	More than 90 minutes

The decision criteria depend upon the current performance of the organisation. Also for night shifts, etc., the call to the manager and above would be first thing the following working day.

For example, as a result of deep safety improvement over many years, as plant president I was called immediately whenever any incident happened, regardless of severity. Go and See was top priority regardless of my planned agenda. This was made very manageable because of the low level of incidents achieved. Personally, following the root cause investigation and permanent countermeasure of each incident gave everyone certainty that safety truly was the number one priority. (Of course, in the beginning, the escalation rules were set at challenging but manageable levels.) To Go and See by yourself does not add maximum value.

The management chain from the place of the escalation to the senior person called should all join at the site, as should the related departments. This way, the very quickest common understanding and authorisation of necessary actions can be made. As can provision of any further support the local people may benefit from. These gatherings are normally no more than 10 or 15 minutes long.

Each escalated item should be followed by the senior level involved to complete resolution. This can require anything between further planned visits to simply a report back at a subsequent daily meeting.

As top management, our role in these gatherings is to ensure that understanding of the issue is based upon facts and that the decided priorities and teamwork are correct.

Make a point of 'getting your hands dirty' by checking personally. Go into details and, where appropriate, try the process for yourself. Ask questions of the people working in the area. This example will initially be a shock for your people, but will clearly demonstrate the kind of behaviour you expect from them. (If the issue is on a manufacturing floor or worksite, be sure to have the correct PPE before leaving the office.)

I promise that you will discover many cases where the 'facts' you heard before the Go and See will be very wrong. By setting the example yourself, the facts of subsequent issues will very soon become accurate because your people will have learned.

Your Go and See is to confirm the standards and process.

The issue you are investigating is just a good way to do this. The hands-on confirmation of the detail will speak volumes about how strong and systematic the management is regarding the issue. This not a test of your technical expertise, your people are there to help with that. Ask rather than tell is the best way, except of course in emergencies when command and control is needed.

A golden rule is never to assume or to allow any assumptions.

These incidents are also a perfect opportunity to coach your direct subordinates, but more of that later.

Go and See can also be triggered by the daily, weekly or monthly meeting information, especially where Pareto analysis of the data highlights the issue(s) having the biggest impact upon the KPI results.

If it is worth following, it is worth you going to see.

ENGAGEMENT TOOL 2B

GO, SUPPORT & COACH

It may be worth having another quick look at the two-wheel diagram at the very beginning of the book.

Remember I said that this concept is the underlying principle which differentiates the Toyota management way from others?

One of the most important meanings behind this is that management's role, in any organisation, is not only to run the business, but also to act as coach and conscious creator of development opportunities for their people. From the boardroom to the workplace, each layer of management has the responsibility to develop their direct supports and to ensure that each successive layer is doing the same.

What does this mean in practical terms?

The technical and job specific skills of the workplace are taught and trained, as needed, to the individuals doing the job. Management does not need to know these.

Some skills are generic. They form the fabric upon which the organisation operates. Examples of these, but by no means a complete list, are:

- Coaching
- Practical Problem-Solving
- Process Memory
- The Andon
- The 7 Losses
- Practical Kaizen Tools

Please don't worry if some of these terms are not familiar at the moment, as they will be explained later.

For these generic skills, the training starts at top management. Each member of the top team learns them by practically using them in the workplace under the guidance of master trainers. (Highly skilled and experienced exponents.)

Again, going back to the two wheels, the topics chosen to practise the skill are selected from the already identified business priorities. (The Business Progress Wheel)

Initial classroom training is given by the master trainers. During the training, each trainee identifies the issue for which they most need the skill.

Each trainee begins to apply the skill and the master trainers review and support their progress at frequent intervals. The master trainers advise only, they do not do the activity. It is usual for the top team to present their completed work to all of their colleagues in a gathering. It may seem embarrassing at the beginning, but if done in the spirit of teamwork, the role of each person in the presentation is to take the opportunity to learn from the good points of each of the other presentations and to appreciate their efforts. No one will be perfect. That is fine. Criticism or derision, in any form, even light-hearted banter, is prohibited.

The opinion of the master trainers, regarding skill level and readiness to coach, is given individually outside the meeting. It is not unusual for some people to do two or sometimes even three cycles of practical application before being comfortable that they can act as a coach.

Bear in mind that this practice should always be applied to an issue which is already a business priority. In this way, there will never be a conflict of time allocation and each practice will bring a real business benefit.

When each top team member is happy that they can effectively use and are ready to coach the skill, they arrange to pass it to their direct supports. At these subsequent layers, the initial classroom training is given by the master trainers, but the issue to be addressed during the practical application of the skill must be agreed between the management coach and their subordinate being trained. (Initially the top team member and their direct reports.)

Progress of each individual is periodically reviewed between the management coach (boss) and the trainee. The master trainers will initially join these sessions and support the coach and the trainee. (They will give their feedback at the end of each review session.) These sessions are prearranged at fixed intervals, and there is always an expected level of progress in using the tool. (Prioritisation is given for the trainee.)

The coach learns as much again from these coaching sessions as they did from their own practical applications of the skill.

At the end of each individual's training, their coach will be expecting to see the skill applied in every relevant and priority issue. The coaching can continue 'on the job'.

The cycle continues of the trainee then using the same process for coaching their own reports in the skill and subsequent OJT (on the job training). The master trainers will identify the most highly skilled at each level who will then become the local master trainers for the next but one subsequent levels. The original master trainers will periodically confirm and support the local master trainers.

The whole process is owned by the direct management line. As you will notice, I have gone into quite some practical detail about each of the topics covered so far. The details are truly important and make the difference between fully realising the benefits of the activity and just 'doing some good stuff'.

At each stage of application, the power of the organisation grows and develops. The ability of the organisation to deliver more quickly, with solid and lasting business benefits, increases exponentially.

Master trainers are available for each topic, even if externally sourced to begin with.

If you feel, as top management, that you are truly too busy to fulfil the requirements for learning by doing and coaching of each topic, please do not be surprised when your subordinates feel the same way. Sadly, they will probably not tell you so. They will participate in the compulsory elements of the training and return to business as usual from then onwards. You may observe some encouraging initial benefits, but the investment will not pay back at anything like it's true potential.

Some people have interpreted the willingness of top management to be trained first as representing the humble nature of good leaders. In fact, as practitioners know, it is simply the way to get the 'best bang for the buck' out of their business. It is a very good personal investment which keeps on giving benefits.

Once the skills are being cascaded, there are many opportunities during Go and See to coach subordinates.

Encouraging your managers to invite you to Go and See examples of their people's activities, which they feel are at a high level or very beneficial for the business, has many layered benefits for all concerned. Their people will be encouraged and motivated, even if they are, initially, a little stressed by the prospect of presenting to you personally. If your reactions are always positive and appreciative, this will soon pass. Recognition by senior management is the very best motivator. There is a difference between recognition and reward. The power of personal, on-the-spot recognition by senior management should never be underestimated. It will also enable you to judge their performance in coaching and the expectation levels your managers are setting for their people. Coaching them in these, one-to-one, immediately after the presentation to you, is best.

Your confidence in your people will grow. They will recognise this and be willing to take on larger challenges. Also, you will start to feel comfortable in setting larger and more complete challenges for them. **Both wheels will begin turning in synchronisation.**

CHAPTER 6

PRACTICAL PROBLEM-SOLVING

ENGAGEMENT TOOL 3
PRACTICAL PROBLEM-SOLVING

WHY IS IT SO IMPORTANT?

Creating the visualisation, using it to steer the daily, weekly, and monthly meetings plus 'going and seeing' will enable the organisation to share common and factual understanding of the current situation and to have common, short-term priorities.

The two wheels begin to turn and improvements to business results will come with each step. But we will still be relying upon the skills which our people already have. It is a good time to look back to the short section on OJD. We still have to satisfy the need for people to be able to identify, and achieve, their own development needs in line with the best business priorities.

Practical Problem-Solving is a very powerful way of doing this whilst delivering the fastest sustainable business progress.

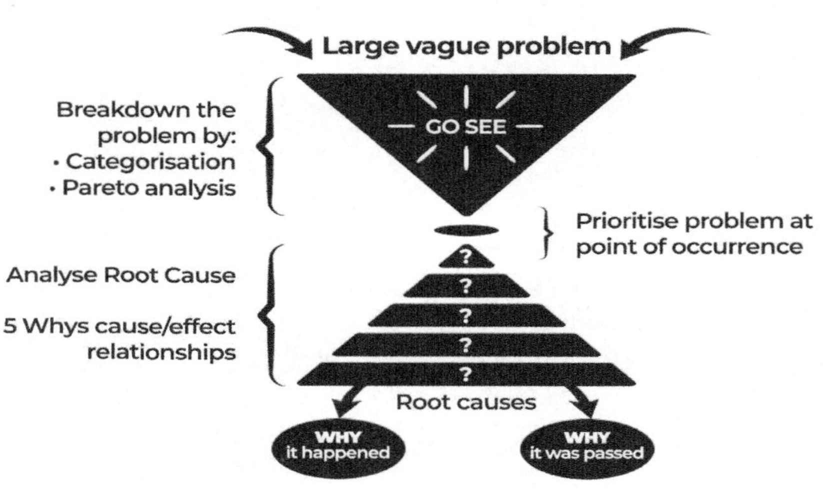

When issues are investigated, to discover the root cause and devise a permanent countermeasure, the participants in the activity will learn the important things needed to guarantee a good result. This will happen when our people truly answer the questions "Which gap in our standard system allowed this situation to happen?" and "Was the gap with the current system itself or was there an issue with the system being followed?".

When our people have invested time and effort into root cause analysis and permanent countermeasure, they grasp for themselves the need for the learning to be embedded somehow so that it does not become lost with time or with changes of personnel. It is the need for the process itself to have the ability to retain learning or Process Memory. *Toyota calls this Standardisation.*

In other words, people's ownership of their processes and their output grows more and more.

Does our organisation have a standard method of practical problem-solving to analyse the root cause and devise a permanent countermeasure? Before we answer that, perhaps let me go into detail about what that actually looks like.

Again, as always, the details are very important! Nearly all organisations have some standardised forms of practical problem-solving, such as 8D, A3, etc., all the way to Kepner-Tregoe and Six Sigma.

They are often seen as complex methods, difficult and time-consuming to use and best left to the few skilled practitioners.

A lot of money and time has usually been invested in training. Their effectiveness largely depends upon the number of people able to use them skilfully and efficiently. Naturally, they are seen as tools to solve complex and difficult performance problems.

If you will excuse me, I will refer to Practical Problem-Solving as PPS from now on.

PPS has the same basic elements as all of these methods, so there is no need to throw away the good money already spent! Using what is already there is the best starting point.

The key skills needed for successful PPS are:

- Categorisation.
- Use of Pareto Analysis. (To find the highest priority and potential benefit.)
- Use of the Cause and Effect/Ishikawa/Fishbone diagram.
- Visualising the system or process to find the point of cause.
- 5 Whys
  (Each is explained in this chapter.)

Again, as with everything, success or failure comes down to the details. What elements are really important in the way the tool is applied? It is worthwhile going through each of the major steps of PPS to make them clear.

When I was taught Practical Problem-Solving in Toyota my first thought was, This is nothing new! *I became frustrated because here was someone teaching me, a 40-year-old general manager, things such as data collection tables, histograms, data analysis and line charts that I had learned as a student! The only new thing seemed to be the fishbone or Ishikawa diagram.*

With practice, it became clear that the elements were indeed the simple ones I already knew. The results came from using them in the correct way and in the correct order.

This analogy applies to so many of the Toyota tools, so I ask for patience when I take your time to explain what seem to be such obvious things in some detail.

I soon realised that I was expected to coach my people in using these tools as part of doing normal business. Becoming proficient in their use myself, by repeated use and levelling up, was not a choice. Thankfully, there were highly skilled practitioners beside me until they were satisfied I was capable.

CATEGORISATION – THE ABILITY TO SEPARATE/CATEGORISE PROBLEMS

Every issue important enough to come to management's attention will be relatively complex.

Example: Our customer satisfaction is lower than we need to secure future business.

As a problem, it is clear and pressing. But if we address it as one topic, we will be reliant upon generalities and exhortations to the workforce to overcome the issue. In PPS, the first step is to break the problem down into its top level subcategories. There are many potential causes for the customer to experience dissatisfaction:

- Quality issues.
- Delivery issues.
- Pricing issues.
- Design issues.
- Packaging issues.
- Environmental issues.
- Poor response to queries.
- Unclear communication lines and so on.

The satisfaction of different customers may vary, from very high to very low.

First level analysis must therefore be to find out which categories of issues are actually contributing to the customer satisfaction problem and for which customers.

This will allow the organisation to work on those things which will add value. But which? The next step is to prioritise.

Some organisations call a meeting and ask the attendees to discuss and decide.

This is a major mistake! Opinion is a very unreliable guide. At every stage of the problem-solving process, the use of facts and data is essential for effectiveness and efficiency. There is no place for opinion or assumption. This is a crucial discipline which will take vigilance and firmness to maintain, but which will pay many dividends from the beginning.

In the example, if there is no data then gathering it comes first, reviewing complaints, survey feedback and customer interviews, wherever factual data is available. From these, a table of impact can be made. I have used number of cases for simplicity.

ISSUE	NO OF CASES
Environment	2
Delivery	18
Price	1
Design	4
Packaging	12
Quality	25
Poor response	6

THE USE OF PARETO ANALYSIS

From this table a Pareto analysis can be made. The Pareto is a much underestimated tool and is very easy to make.

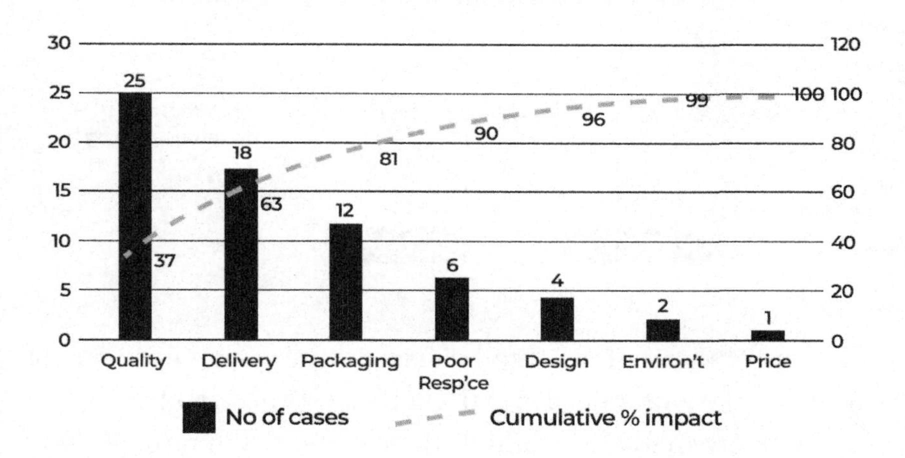

From this one Pareto graph, we can immediately see that Quality issues are the number one priority. By tackling these first, we will have maximum impact on the situation. If we can fix them, we will improve the situation by 37%. By tackling Quality and Delivery, we could improve the situation by 63% and so on. Target setting and resource allocation now becomes very manageable. A similar set of Pareto analysis could be done to find the key customers to address.

USE OF THE CAUSE & EFFECT / ISHIKAWA / FISHBONE DIAGRAM

In PPS, there is only one point at which opinion and imagination are allowable. This is in the construction of the Cause and Effect diagram.

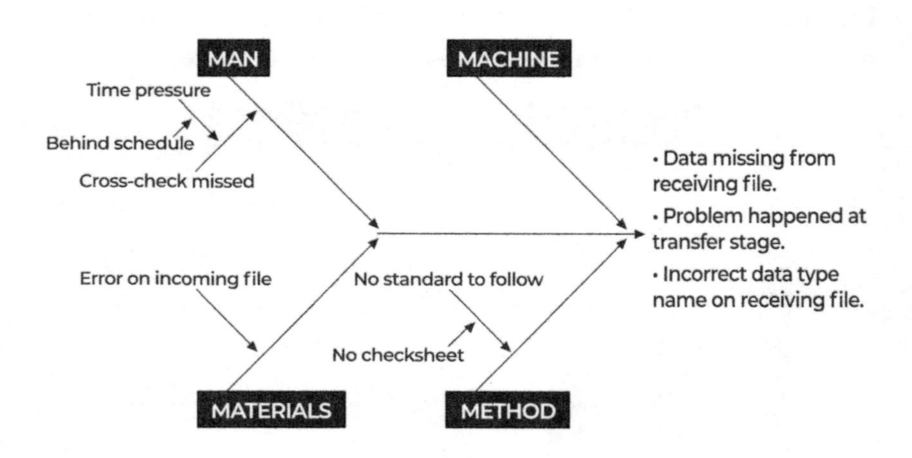

The contribution of potential causes is encouraged especially from anyone with relevant experience and knowledge.

There are many texts about the use of the diagram, but few explain that the efficient use of the tool is directly related to the depth of the definition of the problem in the earlier stages of PPS. The more clearly the problem is defined in terms of what, when, where, who and how (4W & 1H), the more potential causes can be quickly eliminated using just already available information and good logic.

(You may have heard of 5W and 1H, rather than 4W and 1H. The missing W in this stage of the problem-solving process is, of course, Why. Finding why is the purpose of problem-solving.)

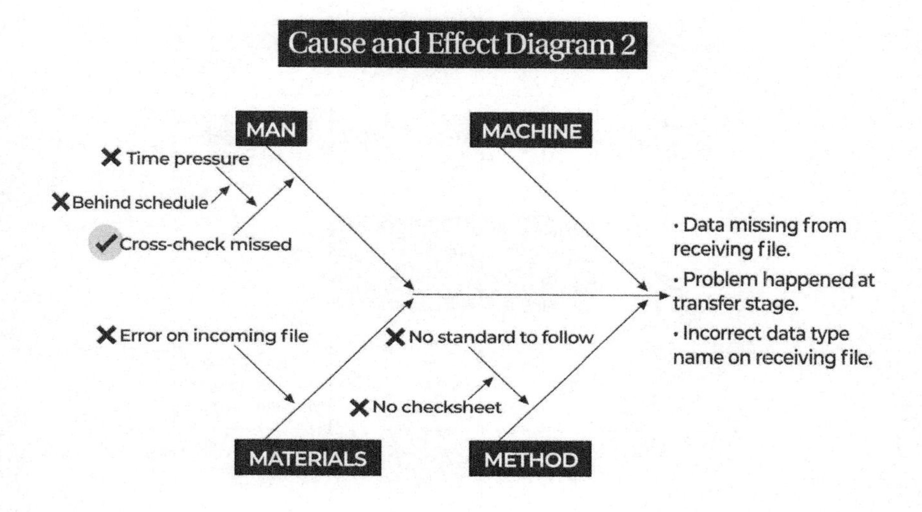

The remaining potential causes can be directly tested at the actual place, etc., and quickly confirmed or disproved.

A small number of true causes will remain, usually one or two.

VISUALISING THE SYSTEM OR PROCESS TO FIND THE POINT OF CAUSE

The easiest way I have heard to describe this element of the problem-solving tool is to ask "What should have happened to make a good result versus what actually happened to make the problem?"

Example: The software package operated smoothly, but some data that should have been transferred from one set to another did not do so. This made the final calculations incorrect.

By illustrating the steps of the process and confirming at which step the defect happened makes the remaining investigation much easier to do and to explain to others.

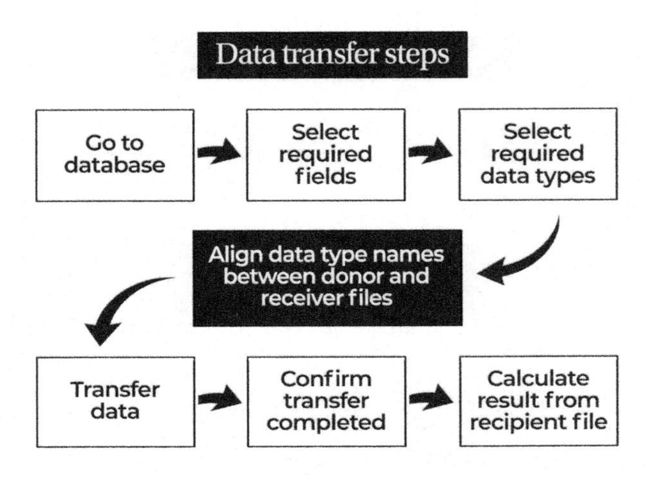

From this point, we have a clearly defined problem with many of the variables of cause already eliminated and we can now investigate more efficiently.

This diagram also generates the thinking about "What are the standard steps of this process?" In other words: "What is our system for this?" We may find that there is no specified method for doing this process, so the first step is to make one, the start of the concept of Process Memory (otherwise known as Standardisation).

At this point, we are ready to move to the Cause and Effect Diagram.

(*Incidentally, many problem-solving processes miss this step and go directly to a cause and effect diagram or its equivalent. The cause and effect diagram becomes very complex because of the number of variables remaining. It is too high level and leads to massive and often unmanageable workloads to investigate.*)

The search for Why (the 5th W) begins with root cause analysis.

5 WHY

This is the least understood but the most important element of PPS.

5 Why investigations follow the actual and logical trail from the direct cause, found by the Cause and Effect diagram, to the cause which, by a simple change in the process or method of working, will eliminate the problem permanently and without ongoing additional work.

EXAMPLE:

Using the same problem.

From the Cause and Effect diagram we have proved the first line:

The standard cross-check of the names of the data types on both files was missed.

(And now the 5 Whys can begin.)

Why?

The staff member doing the job was not aware of this work step.

Why?

The staff member was new to the task and had not been trained.

Why?

Although there is a very clear standard for the task, the training of this staff member was missed.

Why?

There is no method of knowing who is trained in which task.

As you can see, in this case asking why 4 times got to the root cause.

There is no magic number of times to ask why. It is just called '5 Why' for ease of communication. The root cause can be recognised because it is the cause which can be countermeasured by a single action which will eliminate the problem permanently, without need for any ongoing maintenance or extra work.

Here is a very straightforward gap in the management system. A method of making it clear who is trained and qualified for each process is needed. Once this is in place, this problem and many problems with similar causes will be permanently eliminated.

If the 5 Whys had found that there was a system for knowing who had been trained in what, the root cause would have continued until the cause for it not being used effectively was clarified.

There is no place in the PPS method for blame. It adds no value and prevents open communication in the future. There will be a real reason why the system was not followed by the supervisor of the person who carried out the process.

Even if it is necessary to ask why more than 5 times, the root cause must be found.

Business benefit comes from the permanent elimination of the problem.

Development of the people involved happens when the root cause and permanent countermeasures are found by them.

Systematic process management and the real understanding of the need for it grow.

I hear you say:

"There is simply not enough time to do this for every problem!"

or

"Our customers will not wait whilst we do this in-depth stuff!"

You are correct! No, they won't!

We will need an immediate step. Containment action. This will give us the time to find the root cause and take a permanent countermeasure.

CONTAINMENT ACTION

If the problem is a safety risk, is causing customer dissatisfaction, or risks missing an important KPI target, there will be no time to wait for the thorough investigation process to take place. The organisation will need immediate protection. In this case, containment action needs to be taken immediately. Containment Action is expensive, time consuming, hard to manage and maintain but it is great for quickly getting excellent facts and data.

Containment action, often also referred to as a temporary countermeasure, is additional work to stop the problem manifesting itself further. That is to say, the problem will continue to happen, but its consequences will be stopped by additional 100% checks and/or scrapping/rework; whatever is necessary.

Containment actions to protect the customer

- Problem-solving is best in the team.
- Don't hesitate to ask for help or advice from engineers, specialist and supervisors.
- It helps everyone if you show the work on a board.

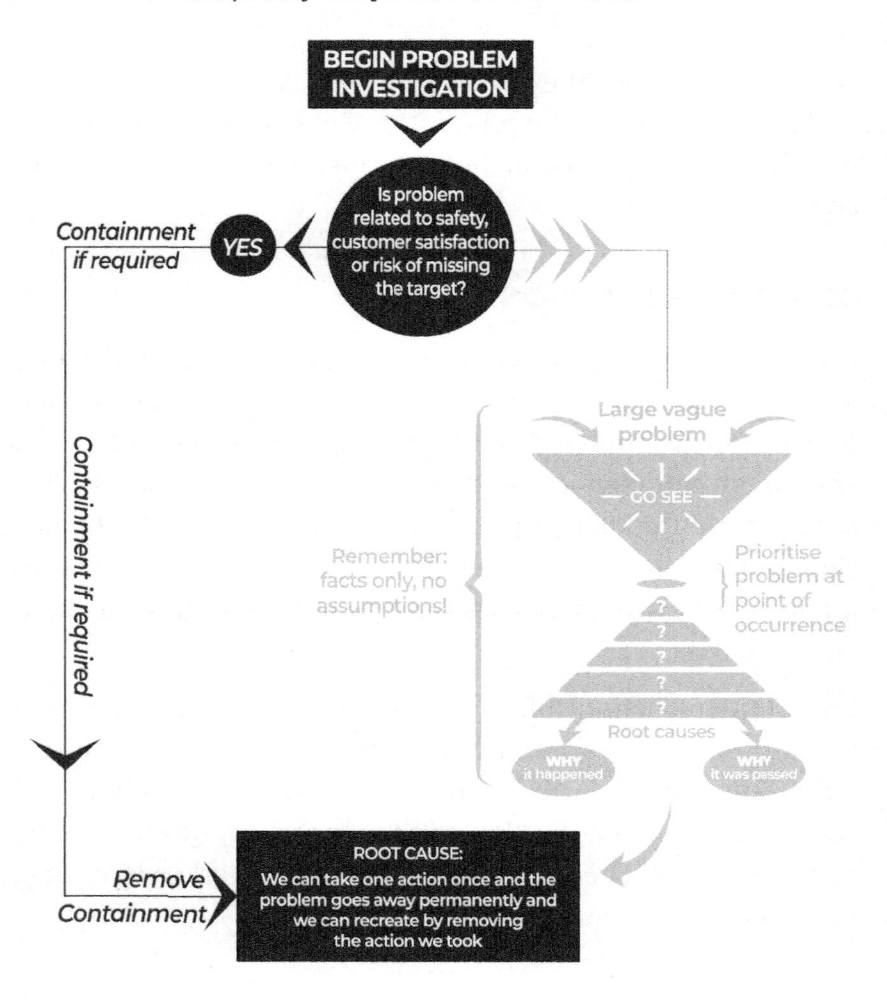

EXAMPLE:

In the example of the software problem, immediate checks of every piece of software under development would be reviewed completely to confirm no similar issues were included. The software at the customer would be rewritten correctly and replaced immediately. Any action necessary to recover lost progress by the customer would be taken. These actions would be done by additional resources, so that normal progress could continue with the planned software development. *(Separate standard from non-standard.)*

The containment actions remain in place until the root cause is identified and a permanent countermeasure is fully implemented.

This additional cost of containment and the additional management effort required to plan, confirm and maintain them are always onerous, but they do provide an excellent incentive for the PPS activity to be carried out as quickly and efficiently as possible.

During the containment action, it is often possible to quickly gather more data and facts, which also help to speed up the investigation.

It is worth emphasising again that in the whole problem-solving process, there is no blame allocated or considered. Top management setting the scene and clearly and quickly correcting any tendency to look for someone to blame is essential.

HOW DO I COACH PPS?

For everyone coaching PPS the principles are the same, regardless of level or position.

1. Learn by doing it ourselves until we are confident we

really understand the PPS process. If it is given priority in our schedules, it will not take long.

2. Focus upon coaching the process of solving, not the problem itself. Let the people working on the problem handle the technical aspects.

3. Ensure each step is followed thoroughly before allowing the group to move to the next step.

4. Set standard review milestones, such as the regular progress meetings. Agree the next review at the end of the current one. (To maintain pace of progress.)

5. Hold, at least, the initial and wrap-up review meetings at the problem place, so we can coach by confirming the facts for ourselves.

6. Strictly confirm that the data, facts and logic being used are sound. Do not permit opinion, previous experience, or leaps of logic to pass unchallenged.

7. Give feedback and opinions only about the problem-solving process itself, not the problem. This is especially critical for top management when we are familiar with the problem topic. Any indication of our opinion will divert the outcome immediately. (Even a facial expression can convey an opinion.)

8. Ensure each PPS activity is well documented as it progresses. This is a treasure for the organisation and is essential to teach the disciplines needed for true root cause analysis and permanent countermeasure actions to be achieved.

9. Ensure as many people benefit from each PPS through the participants sharing their activity with others in their peer group. Sharing during the activity, as it progresses,

is especially helpful for everyone to benefit from our coaching and to avoid wasted effort.

The majority of management follow-up I have witnessed, at all levels, is based upon the solution and actions. “Please report back tomorrow what you did to fix this.” So, speed and ‘doing something’ are the organisation’s focus, which is the buisness progress wheel only.

When the concept of both wheels turning in harmony is grasped, the use of problem-solving as a tool becomes visible.

The emphasis changes from just speed and ‘doing something’ to ensuring that the organisation gets maximum development from each application of the problem-solving process.

OK. “We have too many problems and not enough time to apply this to every single issue we face.” This is very true. It is not necessary to apply the learning emphasis to every issue. But carefully selecting a limited number of the highest priority issues, and taking the time and effort needed to get the full benefit from the tool, pays in many ways.

Firstly, the problems will be solved permanently. They will not recur.

Secondly, the power of the organisation will grow with each experience.

Thirdly, the speed with which the organisation can resolve issues, although slow in the very early stages, will improve exponentially.

Fourthly, if the cascade method, described earlier, of coaching PPS is used, the capacity of the organisation to simultaneously resolve multiple issues grows continuously.

The time, discipline and prioritisation of fully utilising problem-solving can only be generated and exemplified by top management. Taking the personal time to coach is the best method. “It is too complicated for the working level people, they are not able to do it.” I promise you, based upon repeated positive experience, they can and will. More, they will derive enormous satisfaction and motivation from it. The pace and level of business progress/benefit will reflect that. But only when it is a solid priority for you and the top team.

For decades Toyota has used 'Quality Control Circles' as a method of coaching every staff member in problem-solving. Originally QC Circles were the thing that came out of the study of Toyota by external experts in the 1990s. They quickly had a bad reputation, because they were in conflict with the culture of organisations at that time.

I am not recommending QC Circles at this stage. I am recommending the cascade of PPS.

THE CABBAGE PATCH

Making Problems Visible

One of the phrases running through every Toyota facility is ***"You are a manager, your job is not to solve problems. Your job is to make problems visible to the staff members and to coach and support them whilst they solve them."***

A very practical illustration of how this can be done is the 'Cabbage Patch.'

It is a physical display of every defect which a shop or department makes or finds.

It can be a tabletop, or it can be marked out on the floor, depending upon the number of defects and their physical size.

The Cabbage Patch area is marked out by the 5 days of the week and by process or defect type, whichever works best.

This is the original Cabbage Patch for the Forging Division of Toyota in Poland.

Initial Cabbage Patch

Ownership of each defect is clear by process or by defect type and PPS visualisation boards are made by each owner to show their activities and methods.

Each PPS team meets at a set time daily for 15 minutes to follow progress. The supervisors and managers join to support and coach.

As CEO, I would visit a different division each day on a rotation basis, but would stick with one team in each division until the whole PPS cycle had been successfully completed. (Usually 3 to 12 weeks.) The visit was at the team's usual meeting time, and they would present their methods, logic and progress. In the Forging Division the Cabbage Patch originally covered enough floor to park a couple of red London buses!

After 2 Years

By the end of the second year, it was a very small area which seldom had anything on it.

Their problem-solving skill progressed from large volume issues to learning how to find the root cause of problems which resulted in single defects. Sometimes their activities reminded me of true forensic investigations.

They used the internal and external laboratories and machine maker's and material supplier's expertise without hesitation.

The team members learned so much about their processes during that time, and they knew what was needed to ensure good quality every time.

At the end of the second year, the division asked if they could use the Cabbage Patch to improve Operation Ratio (OPR – some organisations use the term OE) and reduce tool costs.

Every production department or group had their own cabbage patch, and every group and team were engaged in solving their issues, one by one, until root cause and countermeasure.

Zero in-house defects became a reality, and customer problem parts were at 30 parts per million by the end of the fourth year of the activity.

The learning was built into new product design and new line introductions.

At the same time, one aspect of Go and See was implemented.

In this case, ***Go and See*** *included making arrangements with our customers to hold any problem for a maximum of 12 hours so that we could get there and investigate it first-hand and on the spot. It was a minimum 4-hour journey to the customer.*

This arrangement required several initial discussions with the customer's president and board and many practical follow-up sessions from our quality people.

Supplier defects were followed and treated with the same pace and intensity.

Did all these things happen because I, as president and CEO, said so?

No.

It happened because the top team and I physically followed the implementation of Cabbage Patch and Go and See every day and for every customer issue for 4 years and every day after that.

The power of our staff members surpassed even our own expectations and they, in turn, were applying the same development to our supplier and contractor companies.

THE UNDERLYING BELIEF

Everyone comes to work to succeed and for their place of work to do likewise.

(I lived through a period up to the 1970s when some people came to work and were motivated by political subtexts, but I have very seldom seen this issue since then.)

Following the steps already outlined will truly get both of the wheels turning.

Top management constantly reminding each other to always consider both wheels in every decision will, in time, make it a built-in habit. Stability will soon become more and more the norm, as the tools and the culture they promote are cascaded throughout.

Because the business progress wheel prioritises the activities, the growth and distribution of the tools happens in an organic way, rather than the classic 'start at one end and work our way to the other' methods of dissemination.

This can be very uncomfortable for top management and for more junior managers nervous about how to report progress.

The truth is that when applied using the business progress wheel to prioritise each activity, the organisation realises tangible business benefits at every stage. There is no waiting until a 'critical mass' of understanding or ability has been reached.

The business benefits will reduce the number of people needed to manage the abnormalities that are currently 'normal'. Taking this opportunity to reallocate the best of your people to promote and support the progress of the tools and culture is now possible and highly recommended.

Let's discuss more about these two topics a little later.

So now we are getting all of the people on their feet and moving! They will be doing good things.

Imagine an organisation like that, where every staff member is sincerely doing what they think is best, but based upon their own limited viewpoint? Will their efforts deliver the best value?

How will they know where the organisation needs to be and by when?

This is the final tool concerned with the engagement duties of top management and is covered in the Direction Deployment section.

Before that, we need to know the concept and practical application of keeping all the learning and development we are getting from PPS. That is to say, Process Memory.

CHAPTER 7

PROCESS MEMORY

PROJECT & PROCESS MEMORY

(Standardised Work / Standard Operating Procedures / Project Keshi-Komi)

At the foundation of the Toyota Production System, as illustrated in the famous TPS 'house', is standardised work.

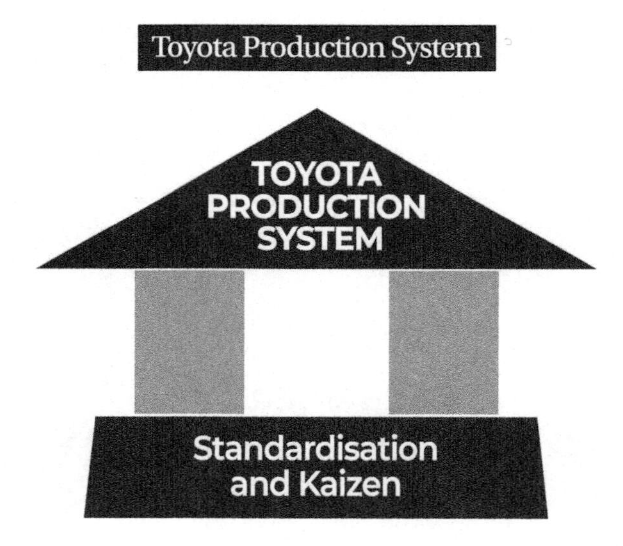

It is explained as: the method of capturing the benefits of kaizen and of ensuring that safety, quality and efficiency are always the best that we know how to do at the moment, no matter who is doing the process.

It forms the documented basis for all process training and is, therefore, the bedrock which enables high manpower flexibility and a true reference point for problem prevention and investigation.

Standardised work is far from unique to Toyota. In organisations that have strong risks for safety, such as the health and medicine industries, the use of standard operating procedures, (SOPs) or protocols, are a basic requirement. Other organisations use them as a formal basis for estimating labour requirements. Very often these standards are prepared by engineers or specialists.

Perhaps a little cynically, my experience, outside Toyota, has been that they are too often remotely prepared and then filed and seldom seen again by the people actually doing the process, unless a compliance auditor visits. Then there is a scrabble to find them. They are seen as a necessary burden to achieve required compliance standards. In reality, there is a strong reliance upon the individual skills and experience of the local people.

Kaizen (process method improvement) happens in all organisations all the time. It is a natural human instinct for a very high proportion of people. If not captured by updating the Process Memory, it just happens invisibly and the benefits stay only with the person who made them. Any associated risks that a 'hidden' change carries also stay with the organisation, of course.

In an organisation at, or reaching, Stabilising, the Process Memory tool is recognised and valued as the property of the people doing the process, whether it is a physical process or an office activity. For example, a new project introduction would be placed into Process Memory using the Keshi-Komi, or the check sheet method. (Please see the chapter on project management.)

Preparing and updating the Process Memory tool is a fundamental part of the activities of the process team. The local, first level leader is normally responsible for ensuring this is always done promptly.

"OK, I get it! Let's start getting all these processes standardised by the people doing them the right away! We only have a few thousand processes, it shouldn't take more than 12 months to get

the first round completed!"

PLEASE DON'T! It will kill progress before it starts and bring slower business benefit than cost. It will also be 'forced' and therefore very hard indeed to sustain.

Your organisation must somehow be managing in other ways already.

Please use the balance of both 'wheels' (Chapter 1) thinking for all the other tools we have introduced. Create and update the standards which relate to the processes your business priorities focus you upon. The same goes for introducing the other tools. Make it a natural part of the introduction.

In this way, the people who have been involved in their local PPS activity will have realised the need for them and the business benefit will be delivered and sustained.

No, the use of Process Memory tools, by the people doing the process themselves, is not a natural progression for most organisations, nor an easy one. It is, however, an absolute prerequisite for true Stabilising and for progress to Proactive level.

In other words, 'built-in' safety, quality, on time delivery and productivity are dependent upon it, as is the sustained realisation of the benefits of kaizen.

The next few pages contain examples of the kind of documents used by office type and shop floor types of processes. With these I will, as always, explain the key points of these methods. Things which are essential to success but which, I have observed, are not always included when the tools are introduced by other people.

PROCESS MEMORY TOOLS

Office Processes

The next three pages are examples of typical process memory tools for office type work.

1. The Introduction or Purpose page: -

   The first or cover page of this type of Process Memory tool explains the purpose of the process. In this case the process is the making of a C.L.E.A.R. Visualisation.

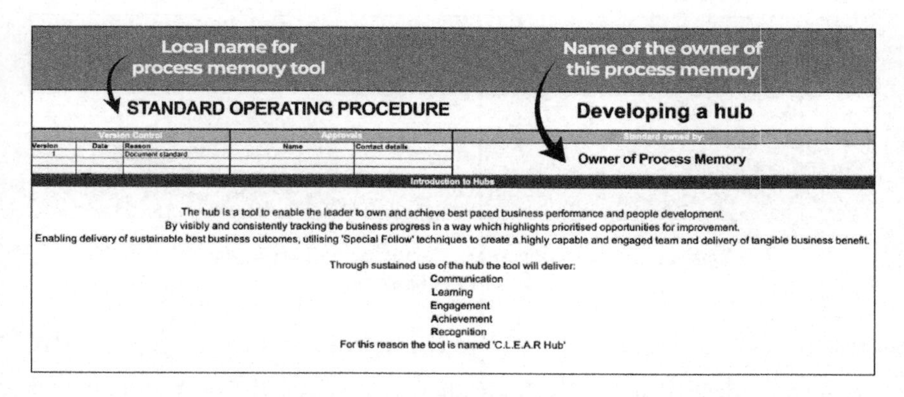

FOR A LARGER VERSION AND MORE RESOURCES, VISIT
WWW.CARLKLEMM.COM

The visualisation has multiple purposes which are not evident from the name of the process itself.

It helps the person studying it to maintain orientation through the rest of the procedure.

Shop floor processes seldom need such a page.

PROCESS MEMORY TOOLS

Office Processes

2. The Major Step page.

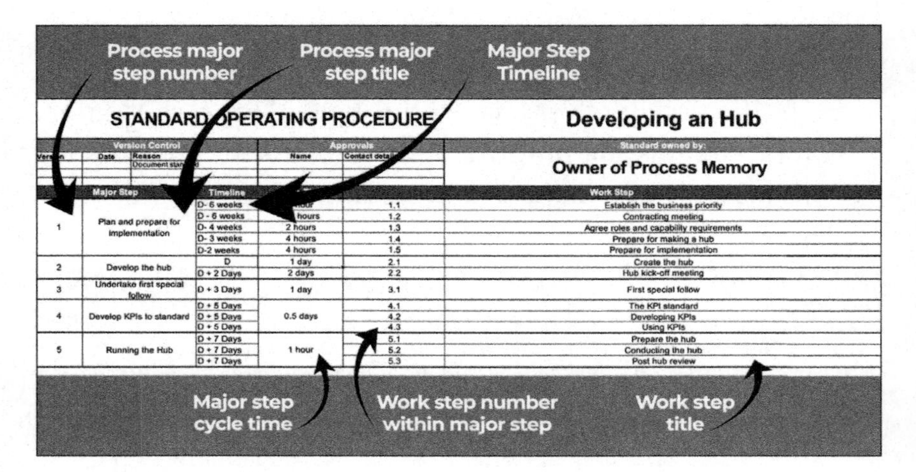

Major Step		Timeline			Work Step
1	Plan and prepare for implementation	D- 6 weeks	hour	1.1	Establish the business priority
		D - 6 weeks	hours	1.2	Contracting meeting
		D- 4 weeks	2 hours	1.3	Agree roles and capability requirements
		D- 3 weeks	4 hours	1.4	Prepare for making a hub
		D-2 weeks	4 hours	1.5	Prepare for implementation
2	Develop the hub	D	1 day	2.1	Create the hub
		D + 2 Days	2 days	2.2	Hub kick-off meeting
3	Undertake first special follow	D + 3 Days	1 day	3.1	First special follow
4	Develop KPIs to standard	D + 5 Days	0.5 days	4.1	The KPI standard
		D + 5 Days		4.2	Developing KPIs
		D + 5 Days		4.3	Using KPIs
5	Running the Hub	D + 7 Days	1 hour	5.1	Prepare the hub
		D + 7 Days		5.2	Conducting the hub
		D + 7 Days		5.3	Post hub review

FOR A LARGER VERSION AND MORE RESOURCES, VISIT
WWW.CARLKLEMM.COM

The major step page shows the top level, or major, steps of the process. Also their cycle time and the work steps which make up each major step. Here the correct sequence of steps is made clear.

In the case of this process, as ir is for creating a visualisation tool, the lead times of each major step prior to start of use of the tool is helpful. These are based upon the organisation structure in which the tool will be based.

PROCESS MEMORY TOOLS

Office Processes

3. The Job Element Sheet

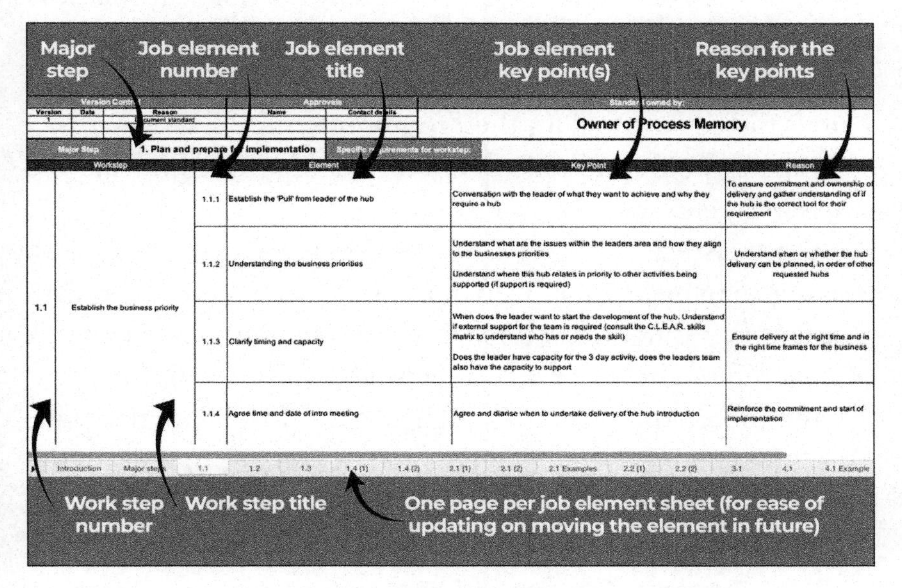

FOR A LARGER VERSION AND MORE RESOURCES, VISIT
WWW.CARLKLEMM.COM

PROCESS MEMORY TOOLS

Office Processes

3. The Job Element Sheet (Cont'd)

The job element sheet shows the individual detailed steps of each work step.

It is the description of how to do the work step and it is at this level that safety, quality and efficiency are built-in to the process.

For each job element there is a space to add the key point(s) for the way the element should be done. In This case the key point of the element "Establish the 'Pull' from the leader of the Hub". (Hub is the local name for the visualisation) Establishing 'pull' means to ensure that the Hub is owned by the leader from the very start of its creation.

For each key point there is a reason for doing it this way specifically. In this case it is " To ensure commitment and ownership of delivery and to gather understanding of if the Hub is the correct tool for their requirement."

The key point and reason are the method of capturing the way safety, etc, are built-in.

These also capture, for example, when a Practical Problem Solving activity or a Kaizen has established that a process element needs to be modified and why, so that there is no risk of misunderstanding or incorrect modification in future.

The job elements are normally held on individual sheets. This is just for ease and speed of modification or moving of the element in future. This is very helpful when work rebalancing is undertaken.

The 3 sheets for the office type of Process Memory documentation are often supplemented by helpful drawings or photographs.

OWNERSHIP

For all Process Memory documentation, ownership is very important. Each process memory must have a named owner. This is usually the local team leader or an highly experienced process operator. All modifications to the process memory must be made or at least authorised by the owner.

In the case of Toyota in the UK, for example, each process is owned by a 'Primary Process Member,' (A Team Member who has proven skill and experience in the process.)

These documents are made by the people doing the process, always. This allows for very quick modification to capture any learning or improvements. Ownership of the process memory is entirely theirs and hence so is the good result of the process.

All training on the process starts with careful and thorough understanding of the process memory. All modifications are retrained to all operators authorised to do the process prior to their next doing it

PROCESS MEMORY TOOLS

Shop Floor Processes

The shop floor Job Element Sheets are very similar to the office sheets.

The authorisation boxes are necessary because the sheets are completed by team members or team leaders and need at least group leader to approve. If more than one shift is operating, the group leaders from each shift will sign before the JES is fully authorised. This is usually done within 24 hours.

Also personal protective equipment will be specified as part of the safety risk assessment the team leader and group leader will do each time there is a change.

These sheets are quite sophisticated and can be much simpler. The use of symbols to indicate, element by element, what are the major impacts, i.e. quality/safety/environment/ cost, etc., is not really essential.

The elements form the basis of the time study sheets.

When I started at Toyota in 1990, the technology was not available for every shop member to be able to make the JES on computer. They were handwritten and each team leader was taught how to make sketches which were clear to understand.

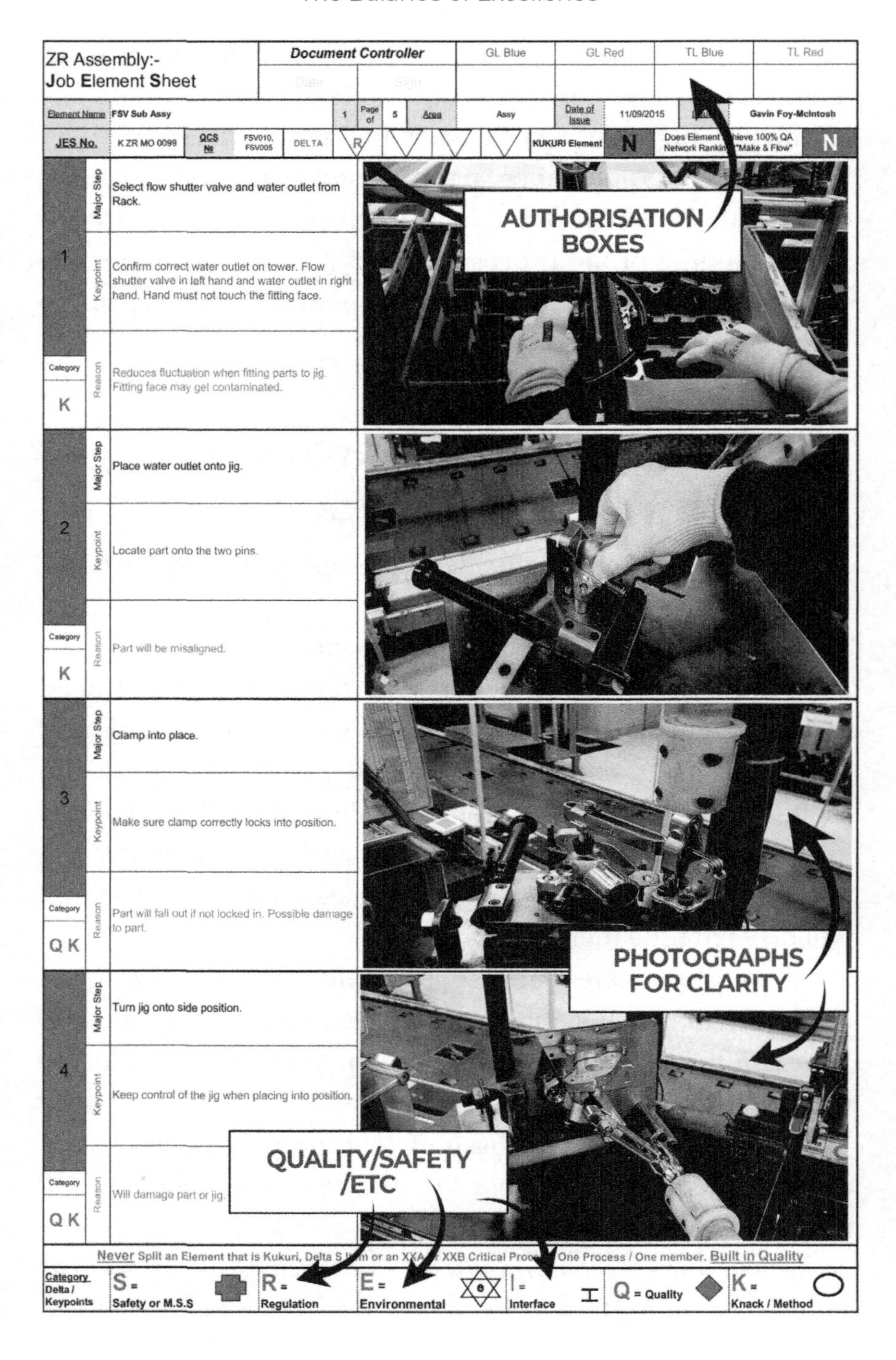

ZR Assembly:-
Job Element Sheet

Document Controller		GL Blue	GL Red	TL Blue	TL Red
Date	Sign				

Element Name: FSV Sub Assy | 1 Page of 5 | Area: Assy | Date of Issue: 11/09/2015 | Gavin Foy-McIntosh

JES No.: K ZR MO 0099 | QCS №: FSV010, FSV005 | DELTA | R | KUKURI Element: N | Does Element achieve 100% QA Network Ranking "Make & Flow": N

Step	Category		Text
1	K	Major Step	Select flow shutter valve and water outlet from Rack.
		Keypoint	Confirm correct water outlet on tower. Flow shutter valve in left hand and water outlet in right hand. Hand must not touch the fitting face.
		Reason	Reduces fluctuation when fitting parts to jig. Fitting face may get contaminated.
2	K	Major Step	Place water outlet onto jig.
		Keypoint	Locate part onto the two pins.
		Reason	Part will be misaligned.
3	Q K	Major Step	Clamp into place.
		Keypoint	Make sure clamp correctly locks into position.
		Reason	Part will fall out if not locked in. Possible damage to part.
4	Q K	Major Step	Turn jig onto side position.
		Keypoint	Keep control of the jig when placing into position.
		Reason	Will damage part or jig.

Never Split an Element that is Kukuri, Delta S ... m or an XXA ... r XXB Critical Proc... One Process / One member. Built in Quality

Category Delta / Keypoints: S = Safety or M.S.S | R = Regulation | E = Environmental | I = Interface | Q = Quality | K = Knack / Method

Now, of course, almost every staff member can use simple publishing software and the JESs are very clear with many photographs.

In plants with many new starters, the JES is often displayed immediately above the workstation so that confirmation of the correct process being done according to standards is very easy for anyone to check. Often the sheets hang from a piece of string stretched between posts. This is another example of visual control.

Even as a general manager, as part of my induction, I had to spend time doing the shop floor jobs and making their JESs.

In Tsutsumi Plant in Toyota City, I was working on the headlamp installation process with the team leader watching me carefully and nudging me frequently when I did not work according to the standards. Most of the time, he was finishing the process for me. After half a shift on the process, I talked with the team leader and enthusiastically offered an idea for a kaizen. He became quite red in the face and pointed out, in no uncertain terms, that until I could do the process perfectly 100% of the time and maintain line speed it was better that I focus on that first! (Well, I cleaned his conversation up a bit to be honest.) Me being a general manager was of no consequence when I was working on one of his processes. I never forgot that lesson.

In the very early days of Toyota, when sales and manufacturing were one organisation, each engineer and specialist trainee had to spend 6 months selling vehicles and supporting customers. In those days, the selling was literally door-to-door cold-calling, and the person who sold the car was the customer's contact with the company. He delivered the new car, ensured the customer was comfortable with all its controls and its quality. He also responded to any customer complaints. Even in those early days, the customer expectations were very high, but not as high as now. Every minor paint blemish is serious grounds for complaint and probably price renegotiation. I was invited by one dealer in Kyushu to join them when a customer picked up their new car. Watching the customer spend an hour going over every inch of the car, both above and then underneath, was educational. Interestingly, there was no test drive. The concept of a functional problem was clearly unimaginable.

Every engineer specialist trainee, in every Toyota plant around the world, still spends between 6 weeks and 3 months working in a production team as a team member, usually in the shop they will later be supporting. When I talked with them, as they graduated to full engineer or specialist status, it was invariably one of the experiences they mentioned and always with very fond memories. The team and group they worked with were often still firm friends.

CHAPTER 8

DIRECTION DEPLOYMENT

This is owned directly by top management

ENGAGEMENT TOOL 4

DIRECTION DEPLOYMENT

(Policy Deployment, Hoshin Kanri)

In every organisation, without exception, best intentions and sincere activities are made by the staff members every day.

At each level, and in every department, their view of the current situation and the priorities are different because of their varying perspectives.

Managers particularly feel pressure to demonstrate the best performance of their responsible areas, often in competition with their peers.

Only top management have chance to see the total picture of the organisation and the current and future environments in which it operates.

That being said, I wish I had £1 for every open-minded member of top management who has confidentially shared with me, "You know, Carl, my people are working hard and I know where we need to go, but somehow I can't quite get the two things to come together as effectively as I need to get the results I know are expected of me. Sometimes it seems as though each staff member, even of the board of directors, has different priorities!"

A practical and pragmatic tool is needed to unite the efforts of the organisation in a single direction with clear objectives and timescales.

Even given such a tool, it is important to remember that larger organisations and those with complex structures can tend to behave in a similar way to a supertanker:

- It takes some time to get up to cruising speed or slow to a stop on arrival.

- It needs plenty of notice, time and effort to change direction.

Speed and agility, in handling changes, are competitive assets.

A clear and practical long-term vision really helps. Young organisations often start with 2 or 3-year future visions. With time and maturity 5, 10, 20 and even 50 years become feasible.

I will never forget one of the Toyoda family remarking quietly to the other, during one of our first meetings with them, "Yes, Europe is a very sophisticated, mature and challenging market for vehicles. We may need 35 years to reach a suitable rate of progress, but we will learn so much from the journey."

A long-term vision provides stability for the whole organisation. Year to year and leader to leader, the organisation is charting its progress on a journey, rather than reinventing itself every time there is a change of leader.

Do long-term visions change? Of course, the route taken must adapt as circumstances change, but the general direction and ambitions do not change so quickly.

The making of a vision will be covered later.

For now, back to the how of Direction Deployment or Hoshin Kanri.

There are two distinct elements to Direction Deployment:

a. Initial making and deployment.

b. Delivering the goods.

Many articles are available about element 'a', so I will cover only the true key points.

I can find almost nothing regarding element 'b'.

(This tallies with the experiences of the majority of organisations I have encountered. Where some form of Direction Deployment is in place there are plenty of documents containing thoughts and even targets. There is usually a very low percentage of actual delivery and even fewer Check Act (from PDCA - plan-do-check-act) reviews of why this is so.)

DIRECTION DEPLOYMENT ELEMENT 4A

INITIAL MAKING AND DEPLOYMENT

This should be called **A**nnual **D**irection **D**eployment, because it needs to happen annually; no more and no less frequently. Done effectively, and with experience, it takes 3 to 4 weeks of company-wide effort.

The timing is also important. Direction Deployment will determine the priorities of the organisation for the coming year and, when fully deployed, will materially affect the distribution and size of budget and resource allocation for that year.

It starts, for the first time, with top management getting together to reach consensus regarding the coming year's key necessities and ambitions for the company. (Consensus means that once agreed, even if not 100%, the whole top team fully support all elements of the direction as if they were their own idea.)

(From the second time onwards, the process starts with a Check Act (PDCA) review of last year's progress versus the previous year's Direction Deployment.)

Products, customers, volumes, costs, employee welfare, environmental impact, etc. Where does the organisation need to be by the end of the coming year?

The organisation is not necessarily structured in direct relationship to the elements of the direction, so the top team must then convert each element into measurable targets which do align with the organisational structure.

It is very useful for the top team to allocate ownership for each element of the direction to one member of the top team. It is the owner's role to lead the element through the whole process to successful conclusion.

Each function/division of the organisation will then consider deeply how their responsible areas can contribute to achieving the direction. The element owner will work with the divisional leaders to allocate measurable targets for each division which will add up to the directional element's company-level target.

At this stage, the division leaders will meet with the element owners and with the top team to confirm their clear understanding of the direction and each element. This is also their chance to 'catchball' (Q and A repeatedly) with the top team. This is the time for any of them to bring their input to the original top team's direction. Input can be made wherever there is new information or data that was not previously considered or where there is a logical discrepancy in the considerations. The 'catchball' is sometimes called nemawashi.

The opportunity for formal catchball, or nemawashi, is critical and cannot be skipped over.

Now we have consensus about which division will contribute what toward the total company directional targets.

The divisional leaders will then hold similar meetings with their managers.

The managers then share the total picture with their departments, and the managers establish a consensus around the allocation of each of the division's targets between their departments, sections and groups.

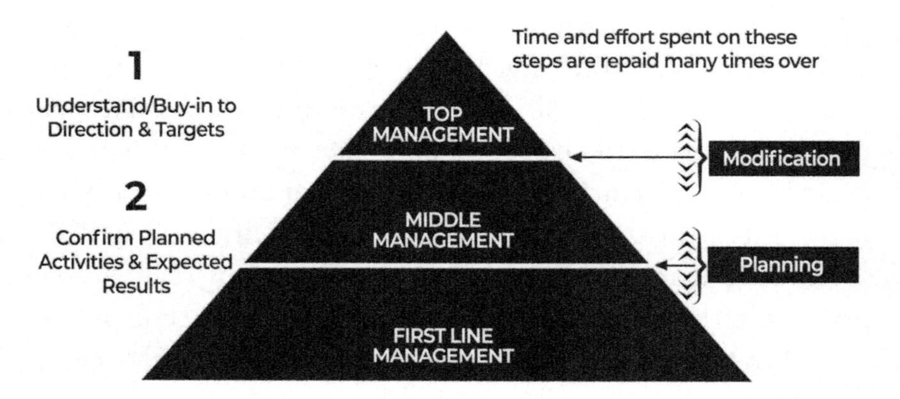

The members of each department hold similar meetings and the targets are allocated between sections, etc.

The sections analyse and brainstorm, if needed, how to achieve the targets.

The targets become the annual targets for their areas of responsibility.

In mature organisations, these targets are then made into real action plans, which are distributed throughout the year according to workload and resource. Pareto Analysis (used in the first stages of Practical Problem-Solving) is very helpful in the setting of priorities, targets and in planning.

Discussions regarding budget and resource allocation happen at this time, along with the opportunity to clarify priorities.

At this practical stage, the allocation targets may need to be revisited and adjusted, as needed, between responsibilities.

The directional company-wide targets are adjusted only after the top team have personally confirmed the impossibility of the original target by Go and See.

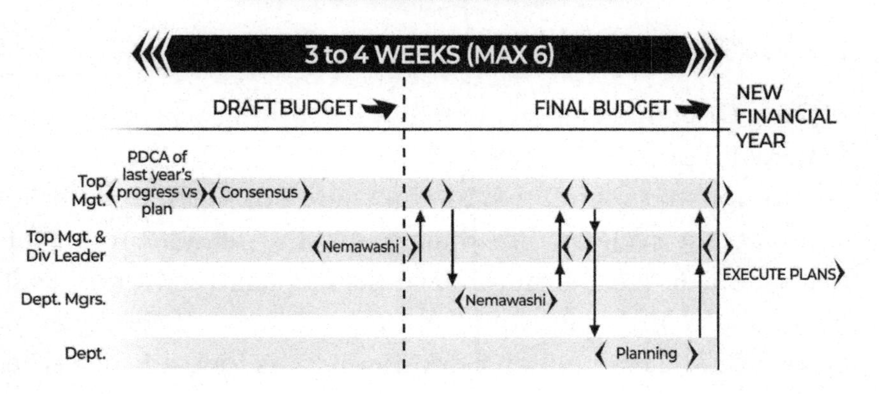

Even in a small organisation, the provision of resource to handle the Direction Deployment process itself has big added value. The more competent the resource the better the results for the business. Planning the process, arranging meetings at appropriate timings to maintain pace, visualising the consensus direction, etc., are make-or-break functions.

In larger companies, this is one of the natural functions of the corporate office.

There are plenty of external resources available to support organisations through these first steps in the Direction Deployment process. I have gone into this level of detail to emphasise the most important elements.

DIRECTION DEPLOYMENT ELEMENT 4B

DELIVERING THE GOODS

1. FOCUS ON THE RIGHT THINGS

Making Direction Deployment, like everything else in life, gets better with practice and experience.

Do not stress if the first attempts are not perfect. Better to complete the cycle on time than to miss the deadline trying for perfection. Judge the number and complexity of directional elements by the maturity of the organisation. If the level of employee engagement and development is low, it is better to focus on delivering less elements but each thoroughly.

Complete the cycles of catchball/nemawashi and agree the targets from company level to department level as the first priorities. This will ensure that there is at least a unified way forward for the organisation and that conflicting priorities are basically resolved. Even for this, in the first cycle ensure at least the top business priority elements of the directions are well done. They will provide a good model for subsequent cycles.

2. CONCRETE AND MEASURABLE

Ensuring that each direction has concrete plans to deliver it is the first step of Delivering the Goods. Each line of the plan needs to have a clear start and completion date and an estimated numerical benefit to a resultant KPI. (With experience in PPS, it becomes practical to do this using first level analysis of the gap between target and actual and using the percentage line of Pareto analysis to estimate the benefits of each focus activity.)

The resulting directional KPI targets can then be incorporated into the standard KPI targets which are followed regularly. (Let the standard system track actual results.)

Ensuring delivery requires following the progress of actions rather than results. If this is not done, there is a very real risk of 'watermelon reporting' in which the KPI reports show a green (on schedule) condition until just before, or on, the actual delivery deadline. This happens right up until the benefit should show in the result, at which point the KPI suddenly turns red (not achieved), and it is too late to recover. (Watermelon = green outside, red inside.)

3. REGULAR AND FREQUENT FOLLOW-UP

Make good and concrete plans to achieve each element of the Direction. These are best made at the working level and in detail at weekly, or maximum monthly, levels.

They provide the basis for accumulated departmental level plans. Again, at a maximum monthly level.

At the corporate level, follow-up of Direction Deployment is at 6-monthly or even 12-monthly intervals. At the plant or regional level 6 months is too long to go between follow-ups.

Monthly is best for most organisations, because it allows frequent enough PDCA cycles to ensure the best outcome.

This does not have to be a long or complex review meeting. A 30-minute stand-up review is usually enough to grasp the situation and to let top management know where their people need support to ensure their success.

SIMPLE VISUALISATION/DEEP ACTIVITY

The simple visualisation below contains all the information top management need to see and inform which enables the grasping of the situation and prioritising discussion time at a glance.

The simplicity of the start and finish timelines are more than enough, provided that the owner has confirmed the detailed planning underneath them. It is very worthwhile for the top management to Go and See the detailed planning at the start of the year.

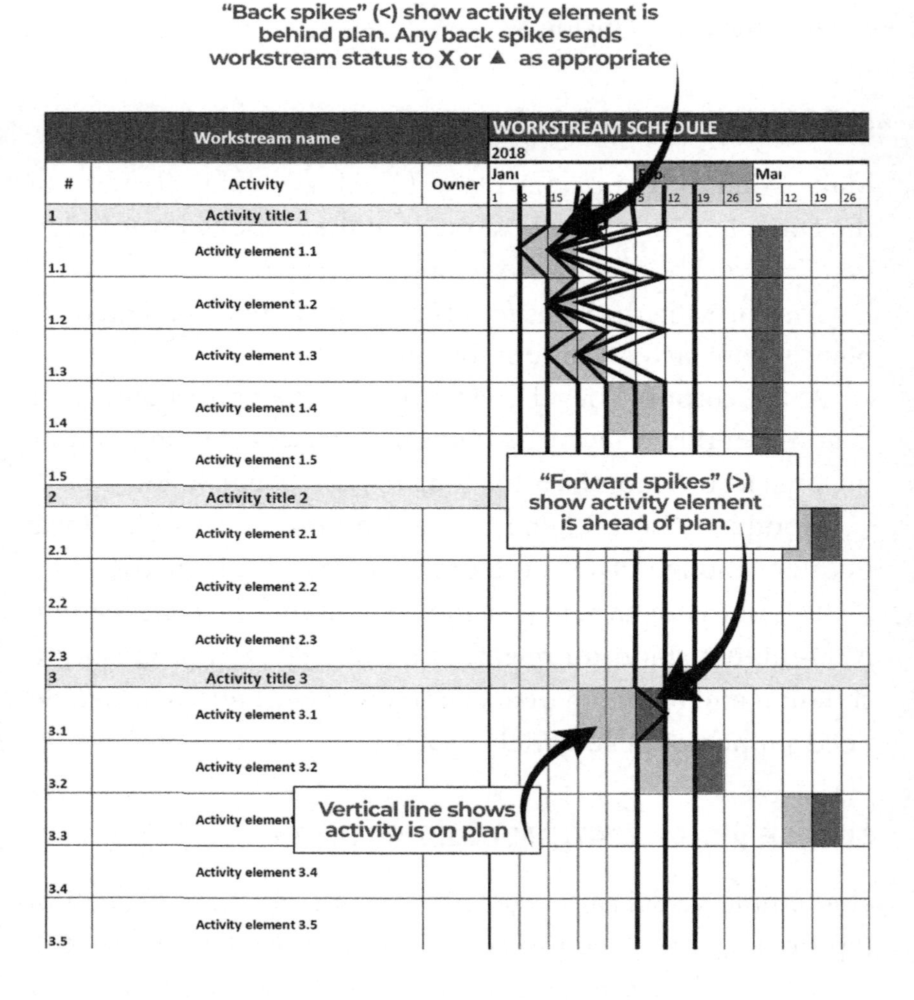

The black status lines show, for each month, what the status versus plan is for each element. The lines simply show where the work is versus plan. They also show, by the length of the back or forward spike, the extent of the delay or advance.

In the review meeting it is normal for the owner of each element to give their feedback in turn.

TEAMWORK

Although ownership rests clearly with the person designated, the leader of the team should take every opportunity to get the rest of the team to support those members struggling to succeed. Please see the notes on 'Andon'.

The minimum monthly follow-up takes a very short time and preparation for it will also be easily manageable if the expectation is clear from the beginning.

Again, please remember that a corporate office type of central resource is very helpful. They can provide the essential reminders to help the development, make new habits, clarify expectations and give advice to help the members of the team to achieve a good standard of preparation and reporting.

CHAPTER 9

VISION AND STRATEGY

This is also owned directly by top management

Having a clear vision for the future of our organisations is a critical element of employee engagement. More than that, it is the tool for aligning all stakeholders.

It provides all involved with the chance to consider for themselves how their efforts can contribute positively to the whole.

To be effective, the vision should be practical and measurable in terms of the business performance KPIs. It should also show not only the end goal, but also the major milestones and their deadlines on the way.

As we mentioned earlier, the more mature the organisation, the longer into the future the vision can reach.

MAKING THE VISION

The most effective tool I have used, with the top team, to establish the starting point for any vision has been the SWOT analysis. It really helps everyone to contribute, and it keeps the discussion in touch with reality from the beginning.

I am sure that most people are already aware of SWOT analysis, so only a brief explanation is needed.

SWOT ANALYSIS

(SIMPLE IMAGE EXAMPLE)

S.W.O.T. Analysis (Brainstorming Tool)

STRENGTHS	WEAKNESSES
▸ On-time delivery ▸ Quality to the customer ▸ Member motivation ▸ Cost management	▸ Big losses during changes ▸ Project lead-time too long ▸ Maintenance achievement vs. plan ▸ Lost time accidents
▸ New technology available ▸ New sales territories ▸ Key customers growing volumes ▸ New product contracts to be won	▸ Competitors prices reducing ▸ Currency exchange rates adverse ▸ High % skilled workforce near retirement ▸ New tech. needed to be future ready
OPPORTUNITIES	**THREATS**

The more factual and measurable the items in each quadrant can be made, once the initial brainstorming is completed, the more useful the vision can become. The gap between the current and the potential future situations being concrete and measurable is the requirement.

The following example below is the vision made by the Toyota UK engine plant in 2005/6.

Vision for 2005/6

GLOBAL CONSOLIDATED PROFIT CONTRIBUTOR

The vision, to become a 'global consolidated profit contributor' by 2011, seems very simplistic compared to the previous SWOT analysis, but the strategy for achieving the vision incorporates all of the elements the analysis highlighted.

There was a clear definition of exactly what global consolidated profit contributor would look like in terms of all the performance KPIs.

The words 'global consolidated' were very important. They opened the door for the members of the plant to work with other divisions and disciplines in ways which would improve their performances, not only that of our own plant.

TURNING THE VISION INTO A STRATEGY

This is most easily explained using the actual Toyota UK 5-year vision example.

The top team pulled together the known milestones already established in plans at corporate and local level. These, combined with the SWOT analysis, provided the framework of the strategy.

For each performance KPI, the gap between the current actual and the vision target was grasped and the methods to close each gap were analysed. The key development needs of the plant members were also established.

A draft image was created, with supporting documents detailing the actual meaning of each of the elements of the vision.

The draft was then discussed (nemawashi'd) with the heads of every related Toyota Europe and Toyota Japan division/ discipline.

Many important new facts and plans came to light as a result of these discussions. Consensus was reached, one by one, with each division and discipline. Naturally, the strategy was modified many times along the way, but the vision was not compromised.

Each of the related divisions and disciplines already had their own priorities and agenda. They were mainly central office functions and naturally felt a strong need to show their leadership and contribution to the plants under their responsibility. As a result, they had developed programmes and strategies which would be applied universally across all of the plants. As all plant heads will well know, not all of these strategies are timely or beneficial to the priorities of every plant.

The clear strategy document we brought to them had a profound impact. They were practically relieved of the responsibility to make their own strategy for us and could happily support the plant's own priorities and direction. Of course, consensus required effort from both sides.

The final draft strategy was then shared with our Toyota Europe and Japan top management team. (Corporate vice president and executive vice president level.) Each meeting required 30 minutes' diary time. These meetings also uncovered important elements of direction which helped to make the strategy stronger.

Here is the condensed top level strategy document.

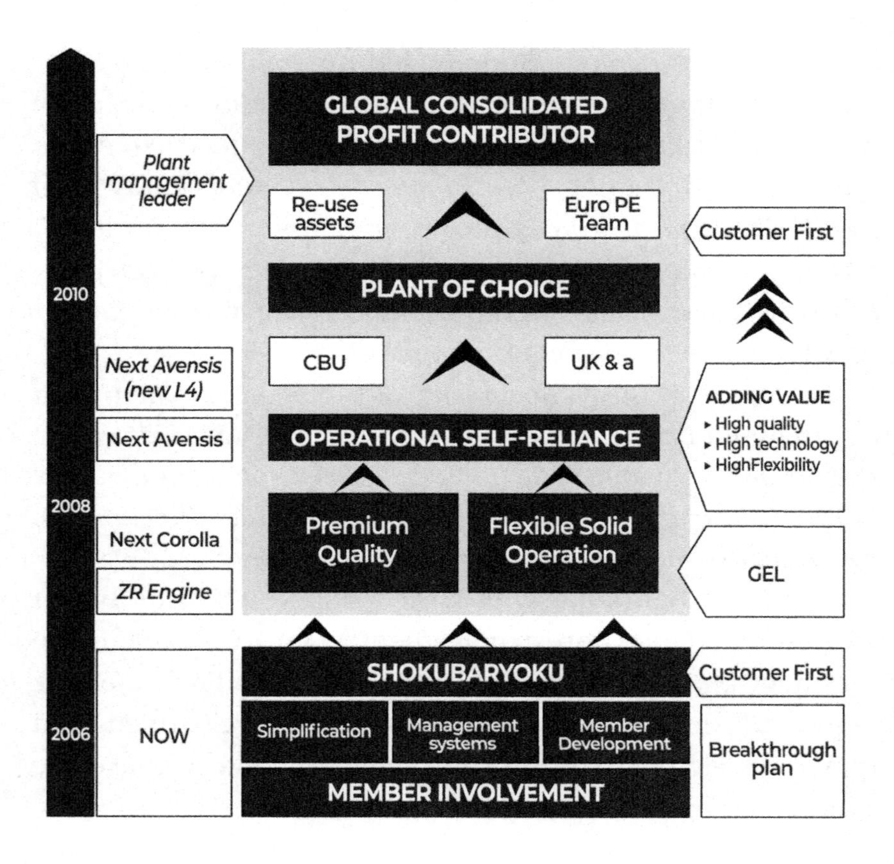

The central pillar (light grey background) shows the objectives at each stage and their realisation point is shown against the black timeline column on the left. The column between them shows the physical projects during the time period, e.g., new models and new engines in which the plant would be directly engaged. The right-hand column shows the management initiatives and programmes which would be utilised at each phase of realisation.

Each objective and initiative was defined precisely. Each

target was concrete and measurable, and each initiative had clear organisation and methods which could be followed against the timeline.

(Please excuse me for not explaining the actual content in more detail. I am sure you will understand why.) Incidentally, in 2008 the global financial disaster naturally resulted in a complete revision of the plant's vision.

I have found that it is very helpful, for all the people involved, in realising the vision if the performance milestones are set to be achieved at the same time as a physical project completion. A new project production start and performance improvement targets being tied together is very motivational. They can both also be managed by one top level obeya (covered in Chapter 27).

REALISING THE STRATEGY

The strategy document and its more detailed subdocuments form the natural basis upon which the annual Direction Deployment (Hoshin Kanri) can be based.

In this way, the milestones are built into the activities and targets of the annual plans.

Not all of the elements of the strategy fit neatly into the standard performance KPI Direction Deployment follow-up system. In these cases, obeyas are very helpful.

Sharing the finalised strategy with all of the members of the plant or organisation at the beginning of its deployment and subsequently sharing the progress at a minimum of six monthly intervals, usually at the same time as the Direction Deployment progress explanation, is a standard well worth adopting.

Equally important is sharing the progress with each of the heads of the related divisions and disciplines, plus with regional and global top management. In this case, annually was usually enough, unless we needed to 'pull the Andon'.

In Toyota the strategies and their progress reports were also shared on a global basis once every 2 or 3 years, depending upon the difficulty and pace of progress required. The heads of every manufacturing company would gather in Japan, or one of the regions, for 3 days to do this. These meetings were attended by the corporate global heads.

CHAPTER 10

THE ANDON

THE ANDON

Creating a Positive Environment

Within easy reach, beside every workstation in every Toyota plant in the world is an Andon cord or button. The member of staff can press the button or pull the cord without having to move from their job. (From now on we will just refer to the cord.)

Whenever anything abnormal is seen by the staff member on the process, they immediately pull the Andon cord and continue with their standard work.

The "virtual" Andon Safe environment

APPLIES TO EVERY TASK AT EVERY LEVEL IN THE WHOLE ORGANISATION.

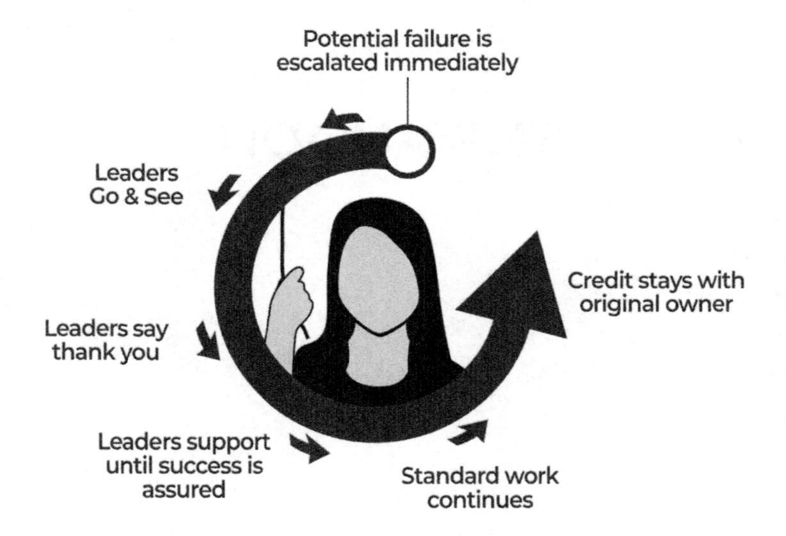

"LET ME FIND MY OWN LIMITS!

They also pull it if they have made a mistake or are not sure that they can finish the process within the specified cycle time.

The cord activates a flashing light over the workstation and also starts a tune playing.

The tune is one which the working team have chosen for their unique Andon. The team leader hears the tune and looks for which workstation light is flashing. He, or she, then goes immediately and quickly to the staff member on the workstation and asks, "Thank you for the Andon, what have you got?"

Whatever the issue is the team leader will take ownership. The line Andon is pulled again by the team leader to allow the line to continue to run and the team member will continue with their standard work. If the team leader cannot manage the issue the Andon is left 'on' and the line will stop at the end of the process cycle time. The group leader will then immediately support the issue. The emphasis is to guarantee safety and so that only good quality is passed to the next process. At the same time, the line will stop only until the situation is managed.

The concept of the Andon is applied to every type of work and at every level in the whole organisation.

The engineer or specialist will 'pull the Andon' verbally to their supervisor if they have any doubts about the accuracy or timely completion of their work.

The manager or director will 'pull the Andon' to their immediate superior if they have any concerns which could possibly delay or jeopardise the delivery of a planned achievement or target.

'Pulling the Andon' is always appreciated and responded to immediately with whatever support is required that will enable the issue to be successfully resolved and the situation returned to a good condition.

This systematic support mechanism has many important cultural and business benefits.

Firstly, it allows the staff member doing the job to focus

upon their work and to maintain the necessary pace of progress, whilst ensuring a good result.

Secondly, it makes all issues visible to the organisation in 'real time,' which means that the exact nature of the issue can be grasped, first-hand and on the spot, by the local leaders. This enables the simplest and timeliest containment and countermeasures to be taken.

Thirdly, the system allows each member of staff to accept challenging targets, without fear of failure or blame. This is invaluable for employee development and the best pace of progress.

In this culture, the biggest sin is for a staff member **not** to pull the Andon immediately if a risk of failure is identified. Not declaring an issue, and hoping that a good situation can be achieved without asking for support, is 'being a selfish hero' at the risk of failure. When the Andon is used, the whole organisation has the chance to support achieving success.

The tools of employee engagement, and the later tools of achieving Proactive maturity, are simple to understand but are very demanding to implement and make habitual. Introducing them without the Andon culture can run the risk of placing an unsustainable burden and stress upon some staff members. Sadly, in my experience, this vital tool is the most misunderstood and incorrectly applied of all.

Here is a personal example of the use of the Andon in Toyota that I will never forget!

One plant, for which I was newly responsible, was truly struggling to meet the customer's demands for volume of product. Members of staff were working very high levels of overtime continuously, including every weekend. Preventive maintenance was falling behind and line availability was suffering. Supply to our customers was at risk. Every member of the plant I talked to was sure that we could not recover by our own efforts. I immediately 'pulled the Andon' to the global head of production. (I made an A3 report to him.) He arrived from Japan 4 days later and saw the situation for himself. Enough production was diverted to other locations to allow a return to a manageable condition for our team members, and a support team, he quickly pulled together, helped us to locally lead recovery and improvement until the diverted volume could be successfully brought back six months later. We calculated that the support cost to the corporation was £8m. There was never anything but a very positive reaction from the Toyota senior management to my Andon.

CHAPTER 11
SECTION ONE WRAP-UP

or

The other stuff we need

WHO CAN CHANGE THE CULTURE OF THE ORGANISATION?

I am conscious that the information in the previous chapters is both at a theoretical level and also in much practical detail. This is not by accident. We, as the head of an organisation, or member of top management, will determine its culture by:

- The way we react to situations.
- The questions we ask.
- The standards of work we accept without asking for more.
- The clarity of our expectations.

If we do not accept allocation of blame, but insist upon a logical investigation of why something happened, the culture will move that way.

If we do not accept opinion or assumption, but rather insist upon confirmed fact and data, the organisation will soon follow.

If our demeanour remains calm and logical, even against raised emotions, and the discussion is always returned to a logical and sensible level that will become the accepted norm.

If we take the few minutes to always Go and See the actual condition of something that we judge worth following, our subordinates will quickly ensure they do so too. Especially if we take them with us when we go.

If the welfare, development and health of our people consistently underpins every choice we make or authorise, the organisation will do the same thing.

Never underestimate our impact upon our people. It is so

much more than is comfortable for most of us to readily accept.

If we do not know what good looks like and are unwilling to stand firm in our expectation of it, including taking the extra few moments to coach, we will get what comes and no more. Coaching requires a clear image of what should or could be. The details explored in this book have proven critical to success over many decades of practice and PDCA, not 'nice to haves' or just 'the way Toyota did it'.

Yes, in the beginning it will seem to slow things down. I say seem because, by using the right tools correctly each time and improving with use and experience, the results will actually accelerate.

"We don't have time to ask our people to do the work again or more thoroughly, there is too much to do," is true if we do not carefully prioritise the topics we choose to learn by doing. It truly is more effective to tackle less topics than normal, but to address them thoroughly and get the maximum benefit.

Once a topic has been chosen to follow, using the tools explained previously, the expectation level must be set by us without fail or exception. That does not mean that we have to be perfect from the beginning. It means that, whenever we are involved, steps must not be missed or corners allowed to be cut.

The three jobs of management

Head work - Heart work - Foot work.

This was explained to me by my first Coordinator, back in 1991, when we were making important decisions.

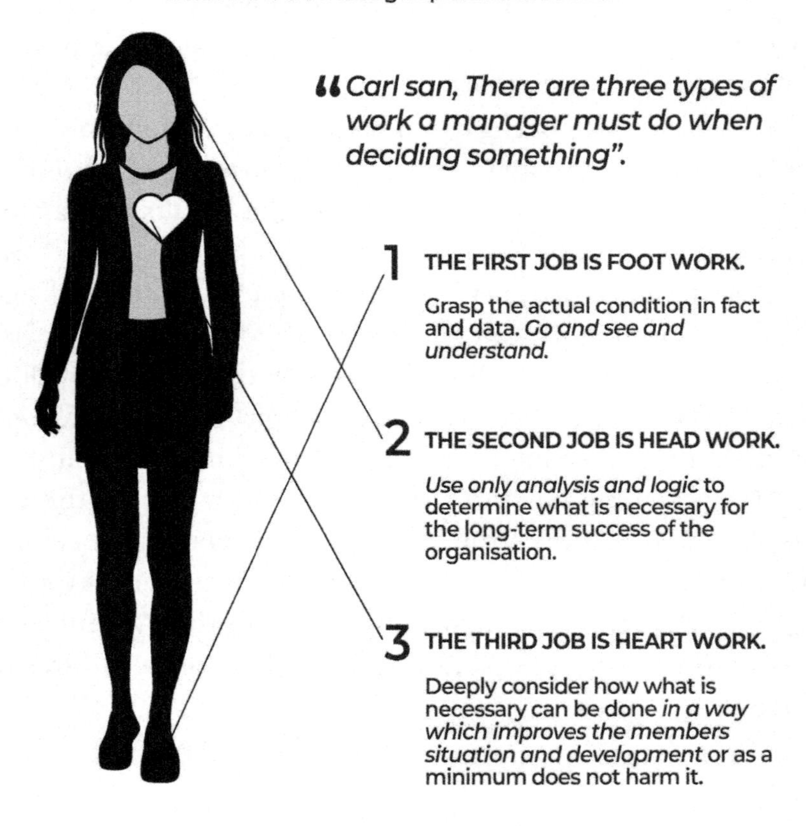

"Carl san, There are three types of work a manager must do when deciding something".

1 THE FIRST JOB IS FOOT WORK.

Grasp the actual condition in fact and data. *Go and see and understand.*

2 THE SECOND JOB IS HEAD WORK.

Use only analysis and logic to determine what is necessary for the long-term success of the organisation.

3 THE THIRD JOB IS HEART WORK.

Deeply consider how what is necessary can be done *in a way which improves the members situation and development* or as a minimum does not harm it.

REMEMBER, OUR PEOPLE ARE OUR GREATEST AND BEST INVESTMENT

COMPARED WITH EVEN THE BEST EQUIPMENT WE CAN BUY THEY CONTINUALLY GROW AND BECOME MORE AND MORE VALUABLE AND FLEXIBLE IN MEETING BUSINESS NEEDS. IT IS OUR RESPONSIBILITY TO ENSURE THAT WE MEET THE BUSINESS RESULT REQUIREMENTS AND DO SO IN A WAY WHICH CONTINUALLY DEVELOPS OUR PEOPLE.

BOTH WHEELS IN BALANCE

LEADERSHIP OR MANAGEMENT?

There is a seemingly endless stream of articles and discussions about 'management' being a negative influence in an organisation, whereas 'leadership' is the best way to achieve success.

From the top management perspective, we are looked to for leadership. If we do not provide clear direction of travel, principles and policies it is very difficult for our people to operate with confidence and without constantly referring to us for our personal approval or authorisation.

An organisation that wishes to delegate to powerful people, at every level, who can move us forward and take new challenges with confidence, skill and professionalism must create the environment and development opportunities in which such people can grow.

Thus the necessity for the second wheel on the axle.

From the business benefit perspective, and to some extent the development perspective, the delivery of activities as planned or results to target in a reliable and timely manner is the foundation of efficiency and success. This can be achieved only through good management control. The PACE of progress is also important.

Wait, did he say 'management command and control'? That feels like the opposite of everything said so far!

No, he said management control. It is having the standards against which our people are able to judge performance correctly. Without it, the ability to 'pull the Andon' does not exist.

Good leadership without solid management control, or disciplined management control without good leadership very seldom brings high-level or lasting benefits.

Being a leader is sexy!

Isn't it…? Doesn't it often provide a feeling of self-worth and power?

Management control at top management level is defined as ensuring and carefully monitoring that the correct level of planning and follow-up is in place and working effectively at every level and process.

Not so sexy! To be honest? A bit of a drudge… "I rely on my managers to take care of that," you might think.

I wonder if it might be a bit of a drudge for them too?

Top management spending time and energy upon the **process** of delivery, not just the result, is essential, providing, by our example, our subordinates with certainty that keeping sound management control is a priority which surrounds everything.

Labouring the point? Absolutely. Because it is one of the most common things top management find very uncomfortable to do. We, at our level, are trained to have short, deeply focused attention spans and minds capable of handling a myriad of issues every day. Taking the time and trouble to ensure solid management control is in place is almost a reversal of everything we have been trained and rewarded for. But the discipline of thorough, repetitive follow through and sticking with the management control process until it is completely effective is part of both wheels.

STRUCTURED ROLL-OUT VS ORGANIC DEVELOPMENT

Structured Roll-Out

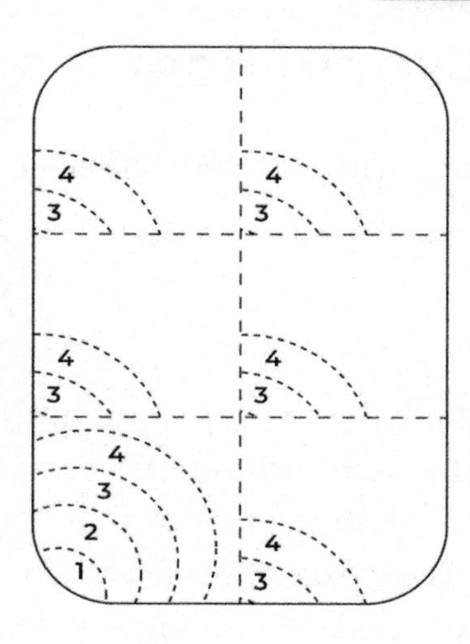

SEQUENCE
1. Pilot or Model Area
2. Expand rollout in same dept.
3. Expand to other departments
4. Expand within all departments

BENEFITS
1. Easy to plan
2. Easy to report progress

DRAWBACKS
1. Management focus is divided between business priorities and rollout
2. Business results are not optimised

DEVELOPMENT WHEEL PRIORITISED

Organic Roll-Out

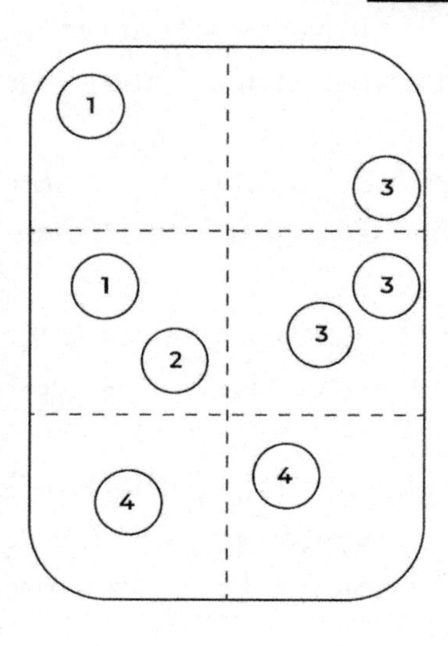

SEQUENCE
1. Pilot or Model Area (Top Business Priority)
2. Expand rollout to next business priority
3. Expand rollout to next business priority
4. Expand rollout to next business priority

BENEFITS
1. No conflict between business priorities and management focus
2. Best business result

DRAWBACKS
1. Planning is more complex
2. Reporting must include business benefits

At each step the participants are the local people plus the leaders of the next step

BOTH WHEELS IN BALANCE

Both methods will cover the whole organisation in a similar time frame.

Organic roll-out is the method Toyota uses. It is based upon business priorities, but drives development. Both wheels are in balance.

WILL RESPONSIBILITIES CHANGE?

Some divisions may need to operate with revised focus or responsibilities than previously.

ACCOUNTING AND FINANCE

As priority issues are addressed, initially by the top team and progressively by more and more of the organisation, the need for understanding the benefits of the activities will grow.

The need to measure the effects and costs of each activity will become important, for the motivation of the employees engaged, for the business result visibility and to support prioritisation and resource allocation decisions. (Also to confirm the rate of business progress improvement.) Often this is supported by a change from traditional cost accounting to a cost per unit method.

Labour cost can then be taken into the total cost per unit and the benefits of using the power of 'surplus' employees accounted for clearly.

The early involvement of A & F in the process of Stabilising will give everyone the best opportunity to learn how this need can be met efficiently and smoothly.

When Direction Deployment begins to mature, there will also be a need to evaluate costs versus benefits in some detail and in advance. A close relationship between A & F and the rest of the organisation will help this greatly.

This is quite a significant change for more traditional A & F leaders. Having time to grasp the importance and the method of meeting this need is very beneficial.

SUPPLIERS AND OTHER CONTRACTORS

During the process of Stabilising issues will become visible from outside the organisation.

It is normal for internal problems to reduce well and problems from suppliers or other subcontracted work to rise to visibility. (In the first chapter of the book we talked about the lowering of the water level exposing new issues.)

The PPS tool helps to educate them and their people in the same way it does our own.

Prompt Go and See by the supplier's people at the problem area in our organisation, plus related staff members of our own organisation 'going and seeing' at the supplier, ensures the quickest resolution and permanent countermeasures. It is also another opportunity for our people to grow and develop their total understanding.

QUALITY ASSURANCE

The quality assurance team represent the customer in the organisation. It is their role to ensure that the correct level of quality is specified clearly. Not too high and not too low. How accurately this is achieved is the measure of their professionalism. Of course, in addition to clarifying the necessary quality standards, they will also work with customer, supplier and design-related divisions to achieve the standards reliably. The responsibility for the in-house-related processes to meet the correct standard must always stay with their own direct (line) management. QA confirms only what they cannot. Confusion about this allocation of ownership leads to many difficulties in achieving and maintaining progress.

Go and See is as essential for supplier issues as for internal ones. When I would visit the suppliers they would initially propose a schedule which started with a presentation over coffee in the boardroom, then a quick plant walk-through. The agenda was always changed in advance to a one-hour Go and See at the relevant area immediately on arrival, followed by a 30-minute wrap-up discussion based upon the facts we had all seen.

HUMAN RESOURCES

The priorities of HR are truly challenged by the changes needed.

Recruitment is modified from emphasis upon an individual's proven skills. The weighting of a proven ability to work successfully as part of a team and to participate in suggesting and supporting improvements is dramatically increased.

The same applies to the assessment of performance and selection for promotion.

Open communication with employees and, where applicable, their elected representatives, sharing the realities of the company's situation, both achievements and challenges, is vital in order to ensure a fully informed discussion.

Most good ideas are not useable in their original form, but can be modified and successfully realised through team discussion and trials often involving other divisions. Based upon this, the concepts employed for deciding the method of recognition and rewards, including any suggestion scheme, may need to be adjusted.

In Toyota, there is no recognition for ideas by themselves. Only the realisation of the resulting kaizen is recognised and/or rewarded. The top team coming to see what has been achieved is the very best recognition. Managers are encouraged and appreciated for inviting the top team to come to their area when something good has been achieved.

Similarly, the manager that supports and encourages their people to present directly to top management, rather than the manager themselves doing so, is highly regarded.

HOW LONG AND HOW MUCH?

So how long should it take my organisation to reach Stabilising maturity and be ready to move on to Proactive?

How much is this going to cost me?

HOW LONG WILL IT TAKE?

It would be very strange for top management not to have this in mind until now, but if it is in our minds it means that we are at least considering the concept. Which is positive in itself.

The answer to the first question depends upon the size of the organisation, of course.

Between 18 and 36 months for organisations between 300 and 600 people can be expected. The most important factor is how we, as the top team, prioritise it as a business strategy and modify our own time and activity prioritisation accordingly.

If we are really determined for "this is how we do our normal business from now on," progress will be quickest.

If we want to continue our current activities and believe it can be installed below us, probably 10 years is not enough.

HOW MUCH WILL IT COST?

With the same provisos as the first answer above, organic roll-out should pay for itself on an ongoing basis by the acceleration in business results it provides.

DO WE NEED SUPPORT?

Based upon the fact that changing habits is painfully hard, I would recommend getting support to speed up the process.

When we started Toyota in the UK, the top team was supported by many Toyota expats, but even so the local top team agreed to support each other with a swift 'kick in the pants' if we found one of us not sticking with the new ways. It really helped.

As progress is made it will be possible to identify activities which are no longer required.

The extra work hours needed to achieve planned volume will reduce as OE (Operation Ratio) improves and stabilises. Inspection will be needed less and rework will reduce. It will be possible to release the best people to support acceleration of progress. This applies at every level of maturity.

MAKING THE TIME!

(I am too busy already!)

"It is all well and good talking about attending stand-up meetings, 'going and seeing,' learning by doing myself, coaching and confirming, but my diary is already full 3 to 6 months in advance. We already have regular reporting meetings and discussion meetings. To be honest, I think the things we are doing now are all necessary. What you are suggesting is completely unrealistic."

That is a completely understandable reaction. Entirely my fault for not explaining well enough.

REPLACEMENT NOT ADDITIONAL ACTIVITIES

The daily and weekly/monthly stand-up meetings using the status visualisation tools will very quickly replace many other review meeting room meetings. In fact, they will be more productive and effective. Each meeting will require less time because the visualisation will allow topics which are performing well to be passed without taking up meeting time. The value-added time can be spent on the areas needing it. Insistence upon sticking to facts and preventing opinions wasting meeting time has a surprising efficiency effect. People will come to the meeting well prepared because the discussion topics will be known to their owners in plenty of time. The culture of no criticism or sarcasm, even in 'jest' will also make the meeting more efficient. That doesn't mean the meetings have to be humourless. They won't be.

The stand-up meetings will, I guarantee, release a lot of diary time. This is especially true when Go and See is used by holding specific topic meetings at the actual place the work is done and involving the people doing it. This will dramatically cut through wasted time on conjecture and speculation. There will be a short period of overlap until the top team recognise the differences and benefits of changing the meetings. Often only a couple of weeks.

The coaching and support happens as a natural part of the activities, they do not need additional time. They are part of how the meeting operates.

PRIORITIES

The subtitle of Chapter 1 is: "Have we been focused on the right things?"

Spending more time focused upon ensuring the priorities

of the organisation are concretely measurable and accurately reflected in the plans of each division at the start of the year will eliminate enormous amounts of time otherwise spent chasing intangible reasons for non-delivery.

The ability of each level of the organisation to use Pareto analysis and clear and firm policies which enable them to prioritise confidently for themselves will ensure the best pace of progress without the need for 'pressure meetings'.

Prioritising our own time differently, allocating fixed and firm scheduled periods each day for us and our management teams to do the things we have been discussing is vital.

Each Toyota entity makes its own decisions about when they do what, but every entity allocates fixed times for a daily meeting at the performance visualisation. Initially 30 to 45 minutes, but this quite quickly improves to 15 to 30 minutes. (There was usually an additional 15 minutes to Go and See any topic deemed urgent or in need of further follow-up. This could be before or after the meeting.)

There is a fixed 15 to 30 minutes to Go and See the actual safety condition and appreciate the work people are doing to daily improve their safety and hazard awareness. For me, this was on a predetermined rotation through the areas. Each of the top team did the same thing in their own areas.

I already explained the 60 minutes daily to do the Cabbage Patch activity. Initially this was quality focused, but as we approached or achieved zero defects the teams changed to whichever was their main priority.

Additionally, 30 minutes was allocated as Go, See and Appreciate time. This could be used by anyone who wanted to invite the relevant top team members to come and see their good activities.

Also 60 minutes was allocated for authorisation meetings.

These slots could be booked by anyone who wanted to explain their proposals. This was always with an A3 or A4 sheet previously authorised by the vice president of their area and after consensus with all related divisions. Each item normally required 15 to 20 minutes. Additional time outside of the normal working day was available if needed. This ensured that top management availability was not a bottleneck to the pace of progress. Each level of the organisation had authorisation ability clearly allocated. Their budget allocation was theirs to control as they wished. Changes of budget, previously planned for a specific topic above 50k euros, required my authorisation. On many days these pre-allocated times were not fully needed, so other Go and See could be done.

These periods were fixed at company level, so that everyone knew clearly the windows for each topic.

Safety, quality, efficiency and cost were managed using obeyas owned by their leaders and 1 hour per month would be allocated for the top team to join their obeya meeting. This was also true for special projects such as new model introduction or major Hoshin activities not covered in the standard meetings.

Once the habit of Go and See has been internalised, not being able to do so is felt as a big loss.

MUTUAL LEARNING

(Yokoten)

Sharing the process of each PPS with our top management peer group is one example of accelerating the progress of the organisation, as is ensuring that our direct reports share their problem-solving actives and methods with us and their own peers. Making a 10-minute slot available at the end of the daily stand-up meeting has worked smoothly in many organisations.

Visualisation is another form of sharing. Circulating the details and learning from each safety-related incident with every member of the organisation is another.

We all learn by experience. Sharing experience with our colleagues is not comfortable at first but quickly becomes normal business if the people with whom we are sharing understand that it is a generosity by the person who took the time to share an explanation. In these circumstances, there is no place for criticism or cynicism.

Every chance to share should be taken and encouraged. I promise it will be time very well invested by all concerned. It is best if it is a standard part of the agenda.

In Toyota Yokoten is a conscious part of the culture. One of my later additional responsibilities was to be the leader of pan-European sharing between the seven plants and also between them and the central functional divisions. It was not happening naturally, even amongst the Japanese expat leaders. The breakthrough came when the accounting and finance divisions in each organisation realised the benefit it could deliver for the business. They acted as secretariat and facilitator between the organisations. Within 2 years, we were realising £2m/year additional cost reduction from the high-level activities. Even group leaders knew and would naturally contact their opposite numbers in other plants if there was a new problem to be solved or a good idea to be shared. I am sure the registered £2m was only the tip of the iceberg and also took no account of the additional speed of progress and learning.

MAKE A HABIT OF ALWAYS CONSIDERING: **BOTH WHEELS IN BALANCE**

To achieve the best and lasting results, guess what sentence Section One must end with...?

Yes, you are right:

It is us, the top team, that first
has to change our ways!

"It ain't what you do it's the way that you do it,
that's what gets results!"

- song by Sy Oliver & Trummy Young 1939

Section Two

MOVING TO PROACTIVE

Moving from Stabilising to Kaizen

CHAPTERS 12 TO 27 COVER THE STEPS FROM STABILISING TO PROACTIVE MATURITY

CHAPTER 12

ARE WE READY?

or

How will we judge that we are Stabilising enough?

WHICH TOOL TO USE TO JUDGE OUR PROGRESS SO FAR?

Moving from Reactive to Stabilising will have delivered many substantial business benefits and developed the workforce whilst doing so. The connection of the whole organisation with the direction the management board decides will also have been established.

No organisation moves uniformly across the board. Different divisions, departments and even sections will be at slightly different maturity levels. It is good to keep moving when an area is Stabilising well. For ease of understanding, the four maturity levels are shown discreetly, but in reality they are a continuum of progress. So we should keep moving forward, as soon as possible, when employee engagement is well established.

Use the listed criteria to judge, as explained in the first few chapters of the book.

Again, it will be possible to decide both specifically and generally.

Stabilising means safety, quality and volume achievement become reliable, that is to say, the daily, weekly and monthly targets are generally achieved or exceeded. Failures are the exception and are clearly traceable to special causes rather than systemic weaknesses.

Process by process, those working with them know what is a good outcome and what is important to guarantee it.

The people doing the process own the outcome.

The Andon culture is deeply established. Failure to 'pull the Andon' is seen as a major failure.

Members of the organisation know where it is trying to go and what their part in it is.

Until now, the focus has been upon getting the foundations in place.

The visualisation, Go and See, problem-solving and Direction Deployment tools being cascaded throughout the organisation are led and coached by knowledgeable top management. The establishment of solid management control provides and maintains the drumbeat, and Process Memory keeps the learning we have gained on the journey. The culture becomes one of mutual support and open sharing.

The power of the organisation to handle multiple issues efficiently, effectively and permanently has grown and continues to do so.

We are ready for the next big step.

THE NEXT BIG STEP

From now we can begin KAIZEN, defined as achieving new levels, rather than problem-solving which is aimed at consistently achieving the current standards. The following diagram illustrates this new level of focus.

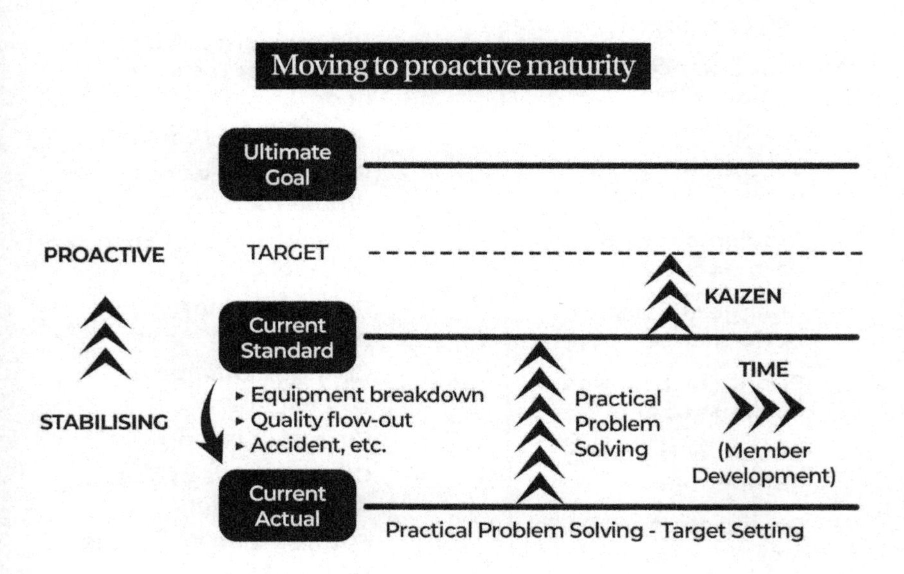

The hourly, daily and weekly variation in performance, in terms of Built-In Quality and output versus plan, will be reducing and staying low.

This is the time to look to the achievement of new levels of performance which, if challenged earlier, would have only resulted in larger variation in performance.

The challenge can also be expanded to include efficiency.

The comparison between Stabilising and Proactive can be seen in the following diagram.

Stabilising to Proactive

TPS Begins

▸ Built-in Quality ▸ Kaizen (7 Wastes) ▸ Planned Maintenence

STABILIZING

PROACTIVE

STABILIZING:

- KPIs steadily improving
- Teamwork improving
- Total process flow visible
- Maintenance becoming a priority
- People are able to contribute more and more
- Problems solved permanently
- Change still disturbs performance
- Priority by best total business result
- Customer is priority number one
- Decisions based upon facts

PROACTIVE:

- Targets regularly achieved
- One team
- Big problem solving capacity at the shop floor
- Seven waste reducing
- Fewer and fewer problems
- Planned maintenance done religiously
- People are more professional
- Changes anticipated and Managed
- Customer is King
- Good analysis of facts drives direction
- Future vision and plans clear to all

The same assessment rules apply at each stage of maturity:

- Use facts and the percentage of the organisation which consistently acts at which level and whether the actions result in performance improvement and staff member development.

- Accept that there will be variation within and between departments and divisions regarding which level of maturity has been achieved. This will happen because the business priorities will have guided where and in which sequence implementation has been done.

- Open assessment, which involves the staff member working in each area, is an important motivation tool.

It will be very tempting to make an assessment check sheet and even get a department to do the assessments. Hundreds of man-hours can be spent debating how to judge the level depending upon the score achieved. Whether this adds big value is uncertain. I have found that, in practice, an open discussion of the items in the diagram usually provides a clear enough picture for everyone to make a working judgement.

Top management does not have to wait for the rest of the organisation to catch up, in fact, it is better to remain ahead. There are many elements of Proactive that are in our hands.

For the role of top management, the three most important baselines upon which to build these elements are:

- Making a 'safe', positive and challenging environment (where every employee can contribute to business improvement and their own development).

- Grasping the (high-level) total material and information flow.

- Learning to practically identify overburden (Muri), unevenness (Mura) and wasted effort (Muda).

These foundations are owned by the top management team. The level of our personal ability and skill in each of these three baselines will materially affect the pace and durability of progress.

CHAPTER 13

A 'SAFE', POSITIVE AND CHALLENGING ENVIRONMENT

I. SAFE

Historically, the members of an organisation recognised that their stability of employment depended upon the fortunes of the business. Hire in good times, fire in bad.

They also recognised that their job security depended upon the method used to realise the benefits of any performance improvements made. (Often efficiency improvements = job losses.)

Hardly surprising when standard business accounting methods clearly show that by far the biggest controllable cost in almost every organisation is labour. *Most of my generation grew up with this as a basic truth.*

Employees, in such circumstances, learned to protect their security by collective strength. Within this environment, any positive participation in efficiency improvement was avoided by the workforce and industrial engineering and work study became seen as an enemy to be sabotaged at every opportunity.

The progress of organisations came to rely upon expansion, technical innovation and management initiatives.

The echoes of these concepts are still strongly influencing many organisations even today.

The concept of employee engagement, as a positive element of every organisation became again very visible when the methods of some of the major Japanese manufacturing organisations were benchmarked. (One of the first studies was the 1991, MIT book *The Machine That Changed The World* by Womack, Jones and Roos.)

In 1987, I was part of an 8-person, senior management study group that were sent by General Motors Vauxhall to the GM/ Toyota joint venture plant in Fremont, California. (The plant had started in 1984.) We were based in a satellite office GM had opened in Fremont which was to be the hub of learning from the joint venture. It was initially manned with production engineers to grasp the technological advances Toyota obviously possessed. Within a very short time, it was realised that there was no equipment in the plant that GM did not already have, but somehow the performance of the plant was far in advance. Within a year of starting up, the office was manned with human resources, production management and industrial engineering people. The 'big secrets' were recognised as the way Toyota thought about people and the concept of the Toyota Production System (TPS). We studied, for some weeks, and went back to implement it in the UK plants. We had some good progress for a few months, by applying the tools we learned, but ultimately failed. It was one of the main motivators for me to respond positively to the approach to become one of the first locals to be hired by Toyota in Europe. I was very keen to see how everything fitted together.

I often reflect upon the organisation of the GM truck plant where I started my training. There was an industrial engineering department. They did all of the time studies and process documentation. There was also a methods study department. These guys were the kaizen team. They knew all about efficiency improvement through elimination of wasted conveyance, walking and motion. In reality, no matter how hard they worked, no one followed the standards in the process documentation anyway. In Toyota, the staff members themselves were either the direct originators or directly involved in every kaizen. They owned them.

The seeds of progress by the employee engagement route therefore landed, and often continue to land, upon stony ground. (This is not to deny that the TPS tools themselves have been introduced in many organisations and, to varying degrees, provided benefits.)

The removal of this 'self-protection' environment opens up many opportunities for the organisation and its people. Practically, it means that employees need to feel confident that engagement in improvement activities, especially efficiency, will not result in job losses.

As a board member it is fair to ask:

"If I can't remove the unnecessary costs after efficiency improvement, what is the point of it?"

There are several practical elements to any answer to that question:

1. **Worth more inside the organisation than outside.** Whilst the organisation is making good progress along the road to full maturity (fully Progressive), there is the chance to utilise any people not immediately needed for the current workload to accelerate the progress and in realising its benefits. Fundamentally, the temporarily 'surplus people' should be more than repaying their cost by the value of the improvements they are achieving. In fact, retaining and utilising these people means that each one will be more valuable to the organisation than the one-off cost reduction their removal would provide. Plus, the avoidance of the cost of future hiring and training needs to be taken into account, and they themselves will develop at an accelerated pace and become even more valuable.

2. **Temporary workers.** Most organisations that experience natural fluctuation in their workload utilise a mix of permanent and temporary employees. The temporary workforce acts as the buffer to absorb rapid changes in workload. The recruitment of permanent new employees

is naturally from the well performing, temporary people. Having a strong core of permanent people enables their development and contribution to progress without pause.

3. **Increased competitiveness.** Increased smoothness of processes plus increased efficiency and reduced costs make quotes for new business naturally more attractive to customers.

   In Toyota, each entity is in open competition with others, including, for us overseas operations, competition with entities in Japan. I say open competition because this did not stop sharing good ideas between us, and we would operate on an 'open book' basis so that costs were transparent within the corporation.

4. **Natural turnover.** Natural turnover, often between 5% and 10% per year, means that 'surplus' manpower will always be constantly reducing. Also, when people become developed, they are able to move on and up by changing organisation. In other words, some of the best people will naturally move on. In the balanced organisation this is not a problem, in fact, it is helpful, because it allows some natural 'convection' to exist internally. The leavers make room for the next group to have somewhere to grow into. Turnover for this latter reason has proven to be at a manageable level, as the majority of employees enjoy the continued development.

5. **Not just labour cost.** Changing the analysis and thinking from cost by each accounting category in isolation to 'total cost per unit' opens up a vast array of cost reduction opportunities which were previously invisible. From design through processing to sales, delivery and customer

service become available. The connection between the disciplines allows much greater collaborative cost reduction.

These elements become increasingly powerful, as the members of the organisation continue their growth and development. Ensuring that both wheels are considered deeply for every decision remains the key.

An extreme experience of this was when the plant suffered a steady reduction of workload from 103% to 67% of planned capacity over a 3-year period.

Having 2000 employees and 5% turnover left a situation where the release of all of the 18% temporary manpower left a permanent 'surplus' of 180 people. Total cost per unit was already well established as an accounting method, plus an added focus of a break-even point was introduced. Enough opportunities for cost reduction by kaizen could be identified to achieve a 35% reduction in the break-even point (to 52% of capacity).

With 180 people available, it was possible to arrange the full management structure to be in place for them. A separate kaizen division was formed, and they attacked every type of cost. Fixed costs were changed to variable costs wherever possible and all costs were analysed for elimination of the 7 wastes. (More of this later.) The target cost reduction was achieved, and the 'surplus' headcount reduced naturally over time. In the interim period, the plant could manage the natural volume fluctuation with none of the normal losses caused by changes to volume and shift patterns. The development of our people was amazing to see!

The plant was one of 7 in Europe, reporting to a central office in Brussels. Purchasing and design were centralised, as was much of external logistics.

Each of the central divisions was trying to support all the plants and had limited resources. Their priorities were, correctly, those of the total European organisation.

The availability of surplus manpower, combined with a clear vision and strategy, enabled me to discuss with the heads of each European discipline the priorities of our particular plant and to offer our resources free of charge and all expenses paid to support their realisation. In this way, we were able to participate in every aspect of a new engine design, purchasing and production preparation. The new engine, with many improvements, would have required a cost increase of more than 150 euros per unit to introduce. By combining our resources and skills, the engine was brought in at the same price as the one it replaced. Our staff members, who participated in the activities, grew in their knowledge and abilities in so many ways. Some of them found new roles and promotion in the central office. Components, which because of special manufacturing methods were previously reserved only for Japanese domestic sourcing, were challenged and the parts were successfully brought into European sourcing giving large savings in lead time and logistic costs.

Could anyone have anticipated the amazing power of our local people? Certainly not I, but the awesome challenge, as always, was a powerful method of developing our people whilst delivering business benefits.

II. POSITIVE

The base premise for a positive atmosphere is that all people come to work to succeed. If every interaction is preceded by this thought, positivity has begun.

It is NOT natural for everyone. Even after 25 years in Toyota, I still have to sometimes remain silent for a few seconds whilst filtering my initial emotional reaction through this concept. Or maybe that is just me?

In practice, it means that blaming someone is not an option. They have done their best, so the issue is one of development, support, or use of the Andon, all of which can be addressed. Ability is also a factor, of course, but in a much smaller number of occasions than the other two.

Too altruistic? Too weak or soft? I assure you, it is not. In fact, when the person involved does not feel that they have done their best, this approach leads them to much harder self-criticism than others would. There is no release by being able to say "The boss was unfair".

The second premise is to ensure that recognition is never missed where it is due.

Where someone has done good work, or strived hard for a challenging goal (succeeding or not), or helped someone else to succeed, their effort should be positively and specifically recognised during normal business. In real time, at the place it is noticed, is the best way.

The third premise is that the attention and interest of top management is already a very positive message for all concerned. The attention of any level of management is positive and should be encouraged and coached by top management. The most powerful form of this is where a member of top management 'goes and sees' at their workplace.

If we encourage our people, especially managers, to invite us to come and see good work or exceptional effort their people have done, there is much added value. The preparation for our visit may take a little effort, which the manager involved should support with advice. The presenter may be initially nervous, which is normal, but this soon becomes a thing of the past.

Remember, though, that these visits are for recognition and

keep any coaching comments to an absolute minimum, if at all.

When our people go home to their family and friends and say "Hey, guess who came down especially to see what I had done and to talk to me today?" it is worth much more than we might imagine.

III. CHALLENGING

A big part of 'respect for people' is the understanding that the people in the organisation have a much greater capacity for contribution than we can imagine. Role, level, and salary are basically irrelevant in this regard.

People respond to being stretched beyond their current comfort zone. It is the stimulus for good development.

It is not uncommon for a manager to limit the challenge he or she gives to their people by what he or she judges is their capacity. It is considered to be 'taking care' of their people. Maybe seen as a 'protective' or 'caring' role? But is this respectful?

I have often been asked, "How do we get people to want to do kaizen? They don't seem to want to." After a brief walk around the area, we can usually find many examples where people have already improved their work methods. Where the improvements are not visible, a brief question to individuals quickly uncovers the same thing.

The improvements were not seen by the organisation and therefore no recognition could be given. The benefits of the kaizen usually stayed with the person who did them, rather than be shared with everyone through improved company performance.

To share a concrete example from back when I was a young

apprentice at Vauxhall Motors, the guys on production would start each shift at their planned workstation on the moving conveyor lines. The experienced operators had made many kaizens to their methods, often involving 'home-made,' special tools, which reduced the cycle time of the work. By the time the first break came two hours later, these guys were 10 stations back up the line. Their ten-minute break time was doubled! This was my first recognition of an almost universal ability and willingness to kaizen if the outcome was positive.

Setting challenging or stretching targets for improvement without any form of support or 'safety net' is definitely not recommended. This is also not respectful. In fact, it is negligent management.

The Andon tool provides a practical and open method of allowing people to challenge, even beyond their own imagined limitations, safely. It gives the ability to say "I am unable to complete the task properly" in time to get help to succeed.

In addition to Andon, the embedding of the other tools, such as visualisation, problem-solving and others which will be explained later, are essential elements of a challenging organisation.

A willingness to challenge currently commonly accepted 'truths' or 'limitations' is to be encouraged, and is also to be carefully watched for in our own thinking.

Not everyone realises that they are struggling beyond their capacity, so it is also the supervisor and manager's role to be able to read the signals. For example, delays to planned progress or stressed vocal or body language.

With these things in place, however, the speed of development of which people are capable has never ceased to amaze me. I cannot count the number of times I have been presented with business and development progress which literally took my breath away.

The pride and sense of accomplishment provided by overcoming a previously insurmountable obstacle can only be available when challenge is present.

RAISING THE LEVEL OF CHALLENGE (MAKING PROBLEMS VISIBLE)

At this stage of development, it is the role of management to go beyond 4S and KPI visualisation in order to make problems visible to the members of the organisation. (Please see Chapter 22 for an explanation of 4S.)

You may remember this diagram from the beginning of the book.

It represents the relationship between resources and the smoothness of working for the members.

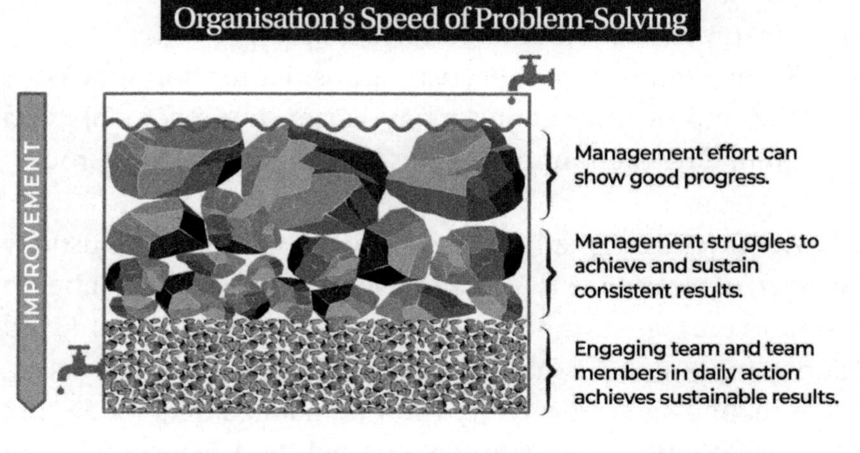

THE WATER LEVEL CAN BE LOWERED AS: demand fluctuates; lead-time reduces; process becomes faster; KAIZEN* increases

AS IT IS LOWERED PROBLEMS BECOME: more visible; more numerous

A high water level, i.e. provision of plenty of resources, allows the work to proceed smoothly even if there are many problems. Problems can be worked around.

Until now, the water level has been lowered by removing the rocks (problems). The problems are identified because they are causing visible losses or disturbance to smooth working.

Once the processes have been stabilised, we need another method to stimulate kaizen. This can be done by deliberately lowering the waterline.

The two taps (faucets), shown at the top and bottom of the tank, represent management's ability and responsibility to control the level of resources available to the members. This can be the number of people, the level of inventory carried, the floor space used, or even the budget allowance provided.

By carefully lowering the water level, a new state of positive tension is created and new problems become visible through new disruptions to smooth performance.

For an example, without creating positive tension, efficiency can be improved by doing many kaizen improvements and accumulating them until it is possible to remove one process from a team.

An alternative method is to remove one member, usually when their workload is low, and using the released member to support the team to quickly kaizen and bring the total workload and manpower back into balance.

Creating such positive tension is management's role and is an excellent way to stimulate growth and development in organisations which have reached a good level of smoothness and proficiency in using kaizen tools.

CHAPTER 14

GRASPING TOTAL MATERIAL AND INFORMATION FLOW

or

The engine of progress

Regardless of whether the output is a product or service, the lead time from customer order to the customer cash being in our bank is a deciding factor for competitive success.

Whether from the viewpoint of customer satisfaction, quantity of income return for effort, or minimum lead times, the flow of the total work is the starting point for top management. We are the people with the responsibility to have this perspective.

TOTAL WORKFLOW

The initial concept is to visualise how the work and information flows through the organisation, from receiving the order to delivering the finished product or service.

For top management, a good starting point is the original, daily visualisation of the total process we made in the visualisation part of the journey to Stabilising.

Remember, this starts with the performance seen by the customer and then traces that performance back, step by step, through the previous processes.

From this start point, we can begin to fill in the actual process time and the actual delivery time.

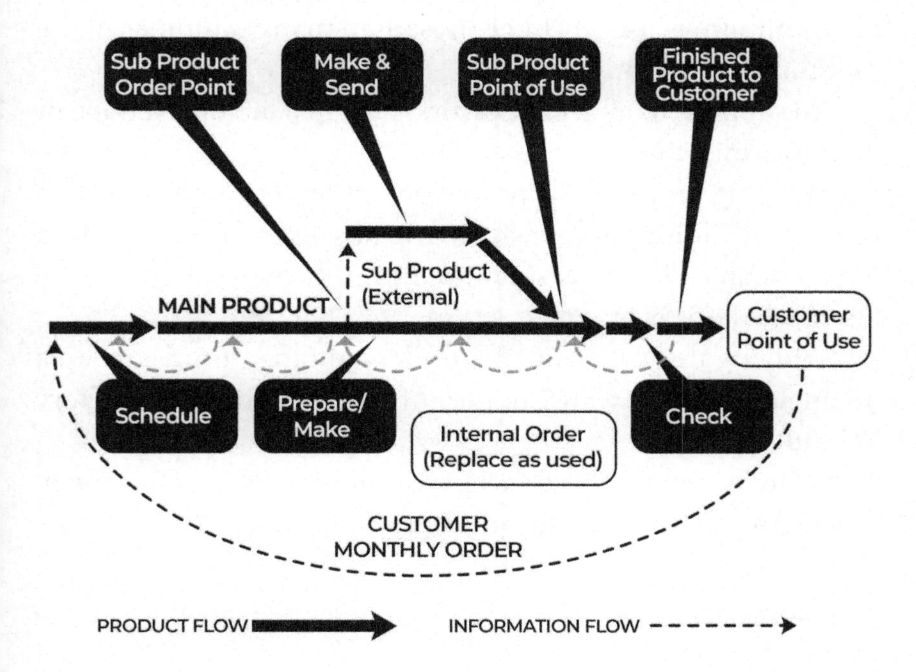

When the total process flow is visualised in this way, opportunities to improve the lead time and the efficiency of the process become apparent.

PROCESSING TIME

The actual time of processing, at each stage of the total flow, can be measured. This is the (ideal) time one piece of work/unit needs to go through the actual work. When this time for each process, in all of the necessary processes, is added together, this provides the current minimum lead time.

ACTUAL TRANSITION TIME

When the actual time for the same piece of work to pass through the total system is measured, the gap between that at the minimum is usually huge. It is often many multiples of the minimum processing time.

This applies to all types of work, be it in a factory, service or other organisation.

Grasping and visualising the actual flow of work, and the flow of the information which triggers each piece of work, makes many of the reasons for these delays, and therefore losses, clear for everyone.

Studying these closely, the understanding of the concepts of single-piece flow and minimum order lead time are very helpful.

At this point, the concept of pull, rather than push, processing needs to be introduced.

THE PULL SYSTEM

This is the most efficient manager of processing resource, regardless of the nature of the work. Starting from the customer order, we do only what is needed, and when it is needed, to meet the agreed delivery date and quantity at the quality level expected. This principle applies for all processes which are involved in the customer requirement. Each process responds to 'pull' from the subsequent process, starting from the final delivery of the product or service and working back, process by process, to the first. Supplies and external service are scheduled for delivery in the same way.

This has three important requirements.

Firstly, it demands consistent, reliable performance of each part of the process. A problem which impacts any part of the process quickly impacts every part. This is why Stabilising is always the first step.

Secondly, it demands real-time management which can respond immediately to unforeseen changes or problems. The members of the organisation need to be able to make local decisions with confidence and to be able to rapidly escalate any issue to the correct level for effective containment to be put in place.

Thirdly, all of the members of the organisation need to deeply understand the importance of their role in the total scheme of the process.

When I joined Toyota, I was told, on the first day, "During your induction and initial training many things will be explained to you. These will be the be the necessary basics for you to function within Toyota. After the induction, you will be given information as and when you request it, we will no longer proactively feed you. If you need information or are struggling to fulfil your role, pull the information from your superiors or the experts. They will always respond immediately and completely to enable you to continue smoothly. If you do not pull the information you will struggle on your own, with all of the stress and risk that can entail.

This is the most efficient use of your time and the time of those around you."

Easier said than done! It took me quite a while to adjust to this expectation. There were a lot of stressful periods. True to the initial explanation, I was never, ever, kept waiting when I asked for relevant information, either from the plant, Europe or Japan. My needs became the priority for those who could help me, and the information given was always complete and clear. That didn't mean I had no need to think. Far from it! Lazy or unclear requests, such as "I don't know how to do this" would be met with the question "First show me your idea, Carl san."

CHAPTER 15

MAXIMISING THE RETURNS

or

Tying up the money for the shortest time

MAXIMISING THE RETURN

(The Engine of Progress)

This part of the book is being written just as the world is starting to emerge from the first phase of the Covid-19 virus.

Most organisations are focusing upon survival rather than expansion. No one is sure how quickly the economy will recover after such a prolonged pause in non-essential activity. Will there be enough cash to see us through it? How to trim our costs to meet the lower levels of business? We know cash flow kills more companies than profitability ever did. We need to get the money, spent in costs, reduced and cycling back to us as quickly as possible.

A few organisations have had the opposite problem, how to increase capacity as quickly as possible. Because of the short lead time, most organisations simply threw money at the problem. No choice, it was containment action that was needed, not root cause and permanent countermeasure. But these companies need to find a way to release as much of that new capital injection, as quickly possible, for success to be sustained.

In both cases, fully realising the value of total current assets is central to success.

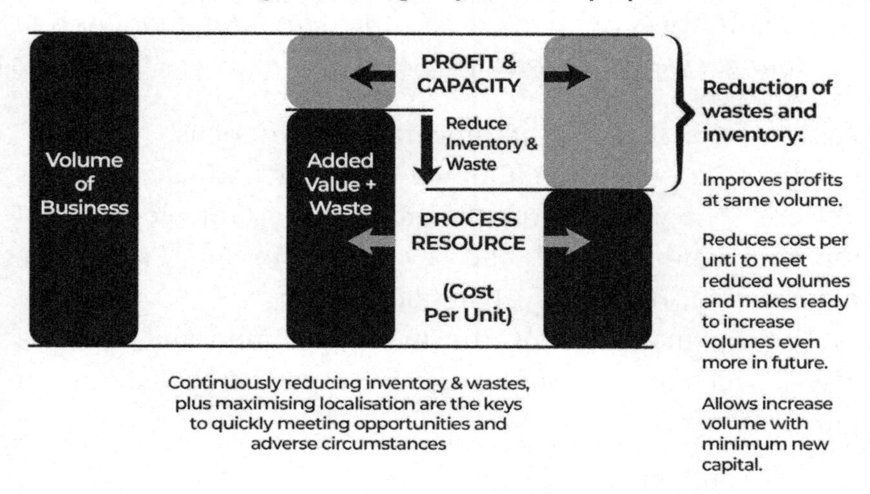

People are central to everything. They provide the power and flexibility all organisations need.

In section one, Stabilising, the engagement and development of people whilst making best business progress was explained.

In this section, the equipping of employees to take the business to new levels of achievement and the tools for them to do so are explained.

Equipping the Stabilising organisation with the ability to use the **tools and thinking way within the Toyota Production System** is the way forward.

From the top management perspective, there are some fundamental concepts which are prerequisites:

- **Speed of turnover.** *Reducing lead times and inventory.*

- **Increasing efficiency.** *Lowering cost per unit.*

- **Minimum investment.** *Using brains not capital. Increasing the output per person, machine and square metre of space.*

- **Flexibility** *to respond quickly and with minimum losses to changes in circumstances.*

I am sure that these are nothing new for most of us.

There are some additional concepts which are less obvious, but which form the most important elements of top management skill and awareness in the Progressive organisation. They are the types of waste.

For top management, the two most important types of waste, which are most often directly impacted by decisions at our level, are:

1. Unevenness of workload. (Mura)
2. Overburden of work. (Muri)

Muda, the famous 7 wastes, will also be covered, but later.

CHAPTER 16

THE WASTES TOP MANAGEMENT DIRECTLY CONTROL

or

Hidden problems we create or allow

I. UNEVENNESS, THE HIDDEN WASTE

(Mura in Japanese)

IA. VOLUME FLUCTUATION

Have you heard this said by an Operations Director?

"Our customers don't pay any attention to the way their sudden changes of order quantity/model mix/delivery dates/ specification changes, etc., cause havoc with our people and systems. We have to keep extra resources in place all the time that we don't otherwise need. We also often have to pay high premium rates for our people and urgent supplies. It has always been the same, and there is nothing I can do about it. They are the boss. If we don't just get on and comply without a murmur the sales division climb all over us at the next board meeting! Sales say their job is to get the business, and our job is to take care of the rest of it. So I stopped raising it."

This is such a normal situation for many organisations that it actually doesn't get raised at the board level, or any other level, except maybe manager and below. Even at this levels they say, "It is just the way it is. Normal business."

Organisations seldom grasp the size of the impact of these sudden fluctuations in terms of costs, management effort diverted from proactive work, stress for the workforce and knock-on impact to the organisations further down the supply chain. The effects pass through the whole supply chain like an exponentially increasing wave, with proportionate performance impacts in each case.

The impact on the whole system's ability to plan and manage with true accountability is also deeply compromised.

Only top management are in a position to grasp the whole

picture and take some preventive action. Ownership of this issue lies with us.

One containment action is building a buffer, where necessary, with additional inventory of finished product to reduce the unplanned impacts for our own organisation and the organisations before us in the supply chain.

Too often accounting and finance controls or a company policy that 'inventory is bad' prevent the managers from being able to do what they need to do.

It is a common, but very terrible, misunderstanding.

Using inventory to buffer 100% of the maximum fluctuation is seldom practical, but even a 50% level will smooth out the majority of the negative impacts.

The inventory brings back the ability to process at standard costs and within plan, which in turn brings back the ability to come back into management control.

This is very important for the whole organisation.

Permanent countermeasures require analysis of the current situation and explanations to/discussions with the customer to establish operating parameters regarding the level of fluctuation which can be managed within certain timescales and the financial impact of exceeding these parameters.

The opposite of unevenness, i.e. levelness, is also important for us to understand.

IB. VOLUME LEVELLING
(HEIJUNKA IN JAPANESE)

Processing products at an even pace, and thereby reducing the losses caused by fluctuation, has substantial impact on every aspect of management and costs.

In the case of complex products with many variants, a

standard planning window becomes very helpful.

For example, if we can have visibility of a customer's planned volumes, even 6 weeks in advance, gives our own planning and scheduling room to make a stable, daily volume and best balance of variants for the processing divisions.

The simplistic image which follows at the end of this section shows the concept.

This levelling has a very positive effect on all departments and all suppliers' costs. Stock handing costs do increase, but they are far outweighed by the other benefits.

This is especially true when the work is then processed in one section.

In the case where the process cycle time of each type of work is different, a mixed sequence, which reflects the levelled volumes, minimises total labour required.

For example

Type of work:	A	B	C	D	E	F
Levelled volume:	10	20	15	30	5	20

Repeated process sequence: DBCFDABCFDDEBCFDABFD in this case for 5 cycles.

SUMMARY:

Stock is held for many distinct purposes. The strict management of the level of stock held at any given time minimises the total costs to the company and permits the processing to be level and smooth

VOLUME LEVELLING BY STOCK MANAGEMENT

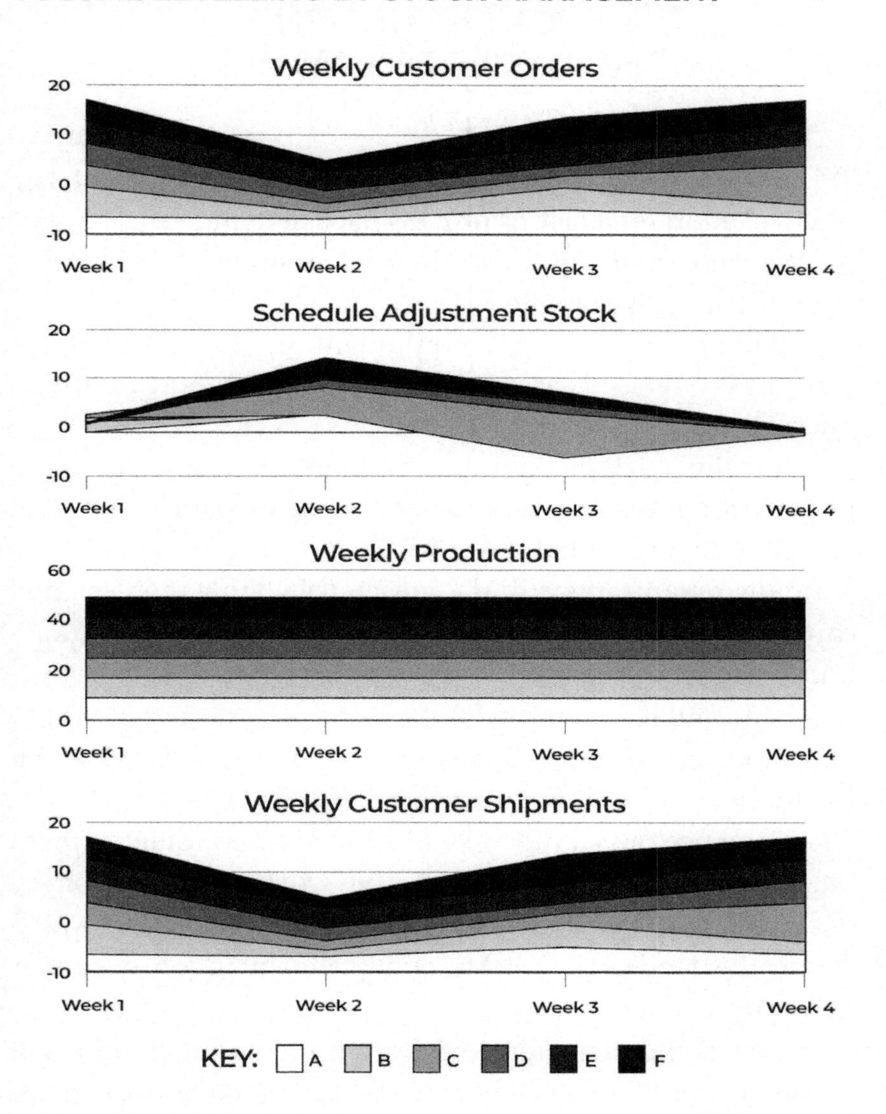

We level the demands upon our processes and also upon our suppliers by adjusting the planned inventory each period, e.g., each week or month. Levelled demand brings the ability to use all resources efficiently and in management control.

II. OVERBURDEN, THE DECEPTIVE WASTE

(Muri in Japanese)

This issue applies to all aspects of resource management, e.g. physical effort for a task or process pace demanded.

The impact of this waste is most easily explained using equipment as an example.

Operating a piece of equipment above its designed capacity is often seen as a quick way of making more return on investment.

Sometimes, it is just running the equipment longer between planned maintenances and sometimes running the equipment at higher than designed speed or force.

Many organisations don't consciously know the designed capacity of their equipment, so the overburden is done unconsciously.

The useful life, in terms of the expected number of cycles, of overburdened equipment is always substantially reduced if we do this.

In practice, it is a little like playing Russian roulette, there may be no visible results for a time, but when a problem comes, it is very often an unanticipated and catastrophic failure which cannot be recovered quickly enough to maintain customer deliveries on time.

As the equipment wear accelerates, increasing numbers of smaller issues of quality and availability begin to arise, with no obvious cause. Searches for 'what changed' are fruitless and frustrating for all concerned.

Top management's awareness of this type of waste is very helpful for the whole organisation.

Confirmation in advance of this risk will benefit in many ways. Smooth processes, reliable output, predictable capital and maintenance expenditure are some examples.

The same principles apply to the people of the organisation. Management need to be very sensitive to verbal and non-verbal signals from their people.

This may, at first glance, appear to contradict the previous explanation of the need for challenging targets to develop our people. Judging our people's capacity in advance is notoriously hard and it their capacity almost invariably much higher than anticipated. In this area underburden is more the common issue!

Please also see the chapter covering respect.

CHAPTER 17

SPEED OF FINANCIAL TURNOVER 1

1. Inventory Management

INVENTORY MANAGEMENT

In-Process and Inter-Process Inventory

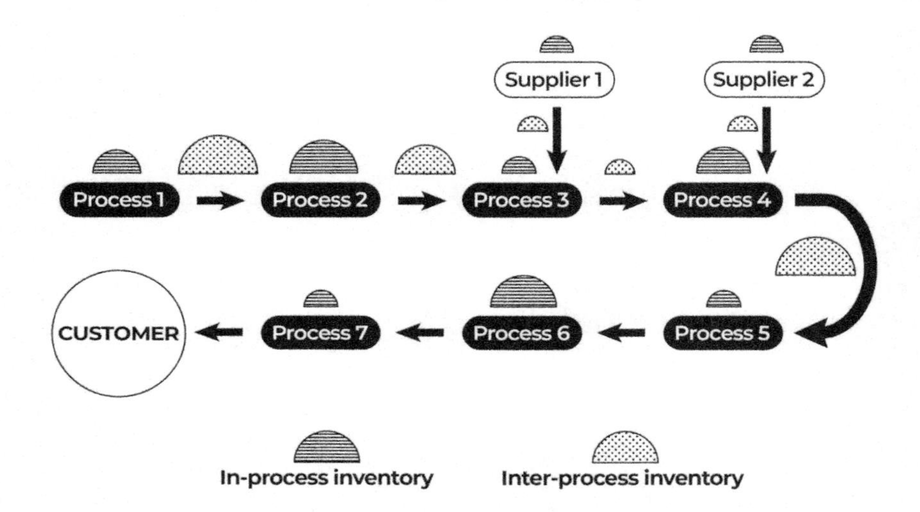

For all organisations, inventory is simply the number of pieces of work. In manufacturing, it can be components. In other organisations, it may be individual parts of a project or even pages/screens of work to be done.

Inventory keeps money out of circulation. It is inherently waste. The money could be adding value in so many other ways.

Inventory makes identifying and handling problems more difficult. If there is a quality problem, for example, the more the inventory the more work must be quarantined and rechecked.

Minimum inventory is, therefore, one of the methods of TPS.

(The ideal is single-piece flow, where the only inventory at each process is the one being worked on and all processes are joined together. Naturally, a pipe dream, but the closer we can get to it, the more money stays in value-added circulation.)

So minimum does not mean zero, it means the minimum necessary for smooth working. Smooth working, in this case, means that the processes are seldom delayed because of lack of parts or internal process problems and never delayed because of lack of a value-added location for the work leaving them.

Of course, if we can connect processes together directly it should be done. (The activities in section one of the book - Stabilising - will be making this increasingly possible by removing many causes of disruption to smooth working.)

If not, then we need to know, what is the correct level of inventory we need to have? This is a standard calculation.

Minimum Inventory = The sum of standard In-Process Inventories + Standard Inter-Process Inventories.

Standard in-process inventory is calculated by the number of pieces/pages actually being worked on at any one time, plus any inventory needed to balance the work because of differences in process cycle times.

Standard inter-process inventory is calculated by the actual time needed to get a component from one process to the next divided by the cycle time of the receiving process.

Once we know the current minimum inventory, we can use it as an ultimate target against which to judge our progress.

Reducing the minimum inventory involves relocation of processes and equipment or is the result of a process number reduction by kaizen.

The level of actual inventory is an important matter of management control. It should never be left to chance.

The necessary level of inventory, to maintain process smoothness under current levels of ability, changes with the circumstances in which the organisation is operating at the time.

Some examples of items which can influence the level of contingency cover inventory needed are:

1. Is the organisation operating a batch process system?
2. Are there factors which make the time taken for delivery transfer to the customer vary? Weather, traffic, vehicle reliability, etc.?
3. Are there occasional quality problems which require inventory to be held and rechecked?
4. Do parts or personnel shortages sometimes delay processing?
5. The customer is known to suddenly change the order quantity during the standard planning period, causing rapid adjustments to planned manning levels, working hours, service or parts supply levels.
6. Projected volume fluctuation is larger or more frequent than can be sensibly managed by normal manpower adjustment. So an average process output volume has to be calculated and inventory temporarily adjusted to smooth out planning.

I am sure the list can be expanded.

Each of such factors can result in problems for the customer. The inventory needs to be adjusted to manage these and make them invisible to the customer.

The maximum inventory needs to allow for such items, and a calculation of their historical frequency and extent will provide an optimum inventory level. Of course, the calculation is strongly based upon probability and several potential factors can often be covered by the same inventory. There is seldom need to accumulate the allowance for each issue individually.

A sensible allowance calculation gives a high level of confidence in guaranteed supply to the customer and smooth internal processes in line with plan.

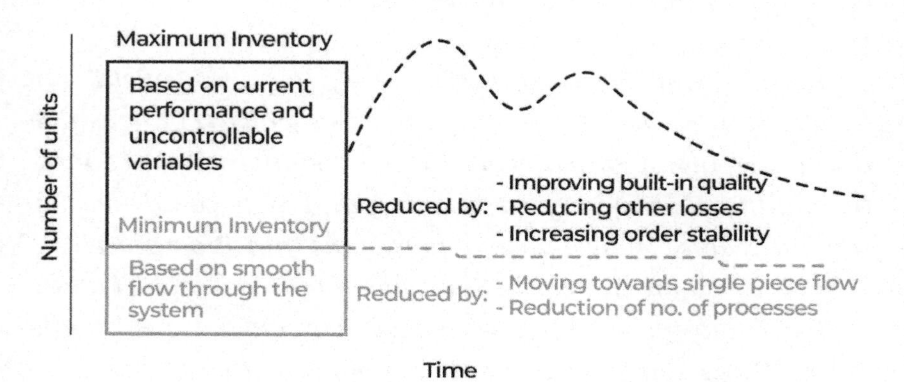

Who operates on minimum inventory? No one I know, because it requires perfect smoothness of every process and transfer between processes. It is an ideal to strive towards.

But every step towards it, by increasing the reliability of processes, reduces cost per unit and the learning from that activity increases the power of our people.

Inventory reduction is initially the result of continuous permanent problem-solving activity rather than a driver in itself.

As the organisation reaches Proactive maturity level, the kaizen activities will reduce the total number of processes needed and hence minimum inventory.

Planned periodic review of the required inventory levels pays not only in the cost of storage, but also allows the **utilised**

floor area to be reduced thereby making more available for new or additional business.

When new plants were introduced into an environment which did not operate TPS, the external unpredictables were often so big that they made operating with low inventory more difficult than in the Japanese home environment. This was an important learning point for Toyota. Adjustments to some levels of inventory, for example those held by suppliers, had to be made.

Even within the organisation itself, for 'brownfield,' not fully supported Toyota sites, the areas in which TPS was first introduced in the company needed to be temporarily 'cocooned' in additional inventory so learning and skill could develop smoothly. This is now a normal part of the transition process.

I observed the same principle when I visited a 'model' plant that GM Europe set up in Eisenach, Germany to learn and teach TPS by doing. (Of course it was not called TPS.) The Corsa model mix was greatly simplified and the supply of components was initially made in frequent and highly reliable rail shipments from the mother plants in Saragossa or Rüsselsheim. These 'mother plants' absorbed any supply and demand fluctuations, allowing the model plant to practise the deeper TPS techniques smoothly.

It worked well and was impressive to see.

CHAPTER 18
SPEED OF FINANCIAL TURNOVER 2

2. Lead Time Reduction

LEAD TIME REDUCTION

What do we mean when we say lead time?

Lead time is the total elapsed time from when the preparation or manufacture of any single product or service is initiated within the organisation until the completed item is shipped or provided to the customer.

The activities explained in the previous section on inventory reduction will automatically reduce the lead time within and between processes, especially if the stock is managed on a first-in, first-out basis.

The tools for further lead time reduction are:

1. Work stream versus department alignment.
2. Synchronisation.

1. WORK STREAM ALIGNMENT VERSUS DEPARTMENT ALIGNMENT

The diagram is a simplified image of the two types of production alignment, batch and work stream.

I have used machines in this case, but the same thing applies to workflow in offices.

1. The top row in the diagram illustrates a traditional production flow, with the different disciplines of cutting, turning, milling and heat treatment separated into their own sections or departments. The system requires batch production to maintain a steady flow of production.

2. The second row shows the same product but this time on a system aligned by work stream rather than department. This enables the four disciplines to operate in a direct flow. (Sometimes referred to as a cell processing.)

Work-stream alignment vs Department Alignment

(Single piece flow versus batch processing)

1. DEPARTMENT ALIGNMENT (BATCH PROCESSING)

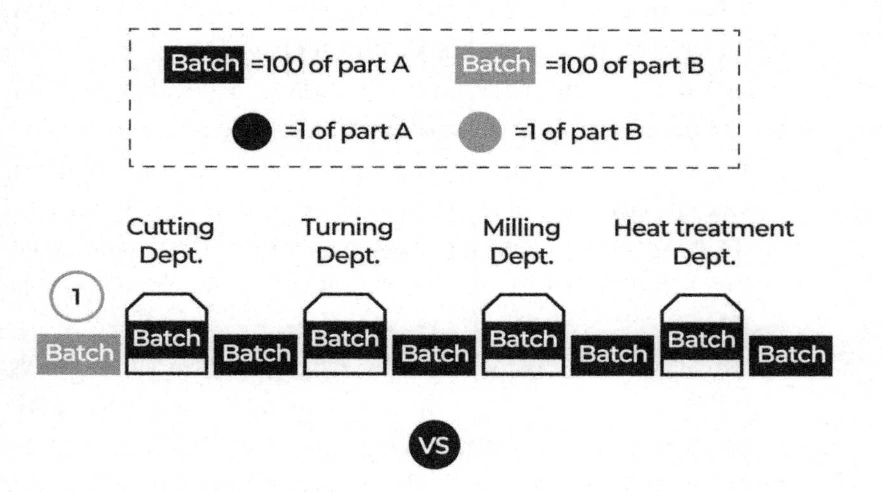

2. DEPARTMENT ALIGNMENT (BATCH PROCESSING)

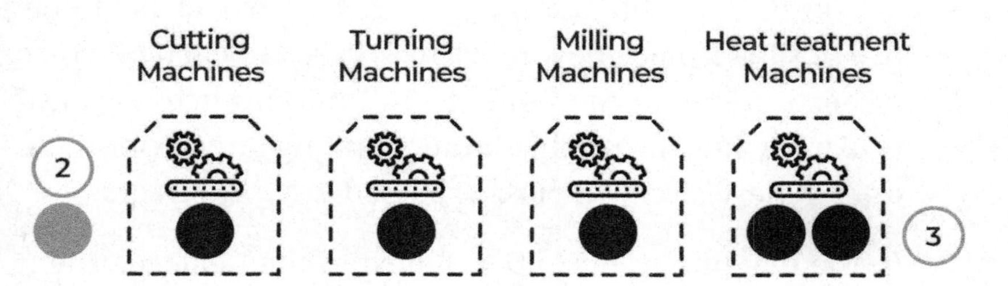

If each part = 1 minute, minimum lead-times are:
1. department align equals 800 minutes
2. work straight line equals 6 minutes

To change from part A to part B, in the case of batch production, needs a lead time of between 100 and 800 units depending upon the work flowing in each department at any one time.

In the case of work stream alignment the lead time is 6 units.

The reduction in inventory costs between the two types of processing is very clear.

The ability to respond quickly to any fluctuation in product or work type is dramatically improved.

The impact of any quality problem is also dramatically reduced if Built-In Quality is in place.

Naturally, the real world is never this simple, but the concept applies regardless of complexity. Lead time is reduced by bringing the processes closer together physically (or virtually in the case of office-type processes).

Joining the processes in a one-piece flow sequence is the ideal method. In manufacturing the inventory is visible.

In offices much less so. The impact of staff members building inventory in the in tray is hidden. Handling work in weekly batches is not uncommon. Work which has to pass through three or four departments can invisibly lose 3 to 4 weeks of lead time.

The ability to encourage, support and expect the timely use of single-piece flow relies heavily upon each person's understanding of the benefits and importance. Physical proximity helps with this understanding and support. So does supervision which is organised by work stream.

3. In the diagram the number 3, next to the heat treatment process, is to highlight that there are two of these machines versus one of each of the others in this production 'cell'. This is because the processing cycle time for heat treatment is longer than for the other disciplines.

   The implementation of work stream alignment will quickly uncover the need for balanced cycle times and managing mixed variations of work type. More of these in Synchronisation.

2. SYNCHRONISATION
(NOT STARTING EARLIER OR LATER THAN NECESSARY.)

As with all of the concepts in Section Two (Chapter 15 - Maximising the Returns), there is inevitable overlap between different elements. In this case synchronisation, inventory and lead time impact and all interact.

The principle applications of synchronisation are:

a. Synchronisation of preparation and on time delivery. (*Just In Time*)

b. Synchronisation of process cycle times. (*Balanced Processes*)

2A. SYNCHRONISATION OF PREPARATION AND DELIVERY/JUST IN TIME

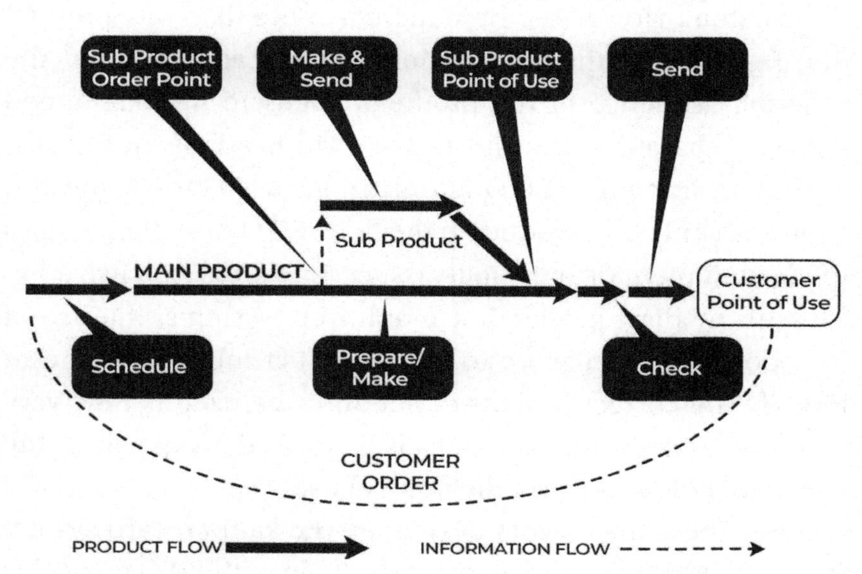

Once we have grasped our maximum and minimum lead times, we can begin to plan so that we do not utilise our cash or facilities any earlier or for any longer than is absolutely necessary.

In the ideal world, we want the preparation of each item and its sub-items, which come together to make the completed product, to begin and end so that they become available exactly at the point and moment that they are to be used.

ORDER LEAD TIME

The order lead time for a product is determined individually by the preparation and delivery lead times. This includes any schedule preparation lead time and any standard inventory.

Visualisation of the product flow and the information flow in such a diagram is very helpful in understanding where opportunities for inventory reduction exist.

For simplicity, I have not shown standard inventory on the diagram. However, where there is more than one product flowing through the preparation process at one time, the ordering sequence of the products needs to be maintained during preparation, delivery and use within all the inventory.

First in, first out, or FIFO, is a term often used to describe this. Even with only one product in the flow, FIFO discipline makes the containment of any quality issues much less expensive.

With modern production monitoring systems, the use of transponders or software to track product movement and to identify the correct process variation to be used is now very common. These systems can also be used to generate the reordering of products at the point of use.

Over the years, Toyota developed the kanban card system to do the reordering manually and to help with FIFO control.

In Japan, the suppliers built their facilities very close to the customer plants and Toyota built their plants close to each other. This meant that the kanban card did not take long to get back to the supplier and order lead time was small. A physical card was fine.

In the USA and Europe, the suppliers were generally well established and clustered around their existing clients. In some cases, the physical kanban would take several days to get back to the supplier, especially when it travelled back on the delivery transport as was the standard in Japan. To overcome this, Toyota kept the kanban principle but moved to an electronic version for externally made parts. The order information flow was almost immediate and the lead time reduced accordingly. (An example of big kaizen.)

TRANSPORTING OF PHYSICAL PRODUCTS

With physical products, there is a need to accept that most external and some internal transportation usually requires more than one part per package to be viable.

The small spaces between processes, which are needed for single-piece flow, also require packaging which fits into the layout and which can be safely and easily handled manually.

Transport packaging, therefore, starts its design by meeting the needs of the end user in size and handleability.

Most current transport is done by truck or container. These are most efficient when maximum space is utilised on each journey. Therefore, the ability of all packaging to efficiently 'cube up' to fill the container or truck is the second design basic.

Protection of the product and ease of removal for use are prerequisites.

The more detailed packaging design required to ensure the

same process cycle time, every time, has further requirements, but these can be covered later when we talk about elimination of the 7 wastes.

2B. SYNCHRONISATION OF PROCESS CYCLE TIMES (BALANCED PROCESSES)

Where several processes are connected through single item flow, the cycle time of each process becomes critical in achieving efficiency. The slowest process (longest cycle time) is automatically a bottleneck.

A quicker process (which has a lower cycle time) than the one following it immediately incurs waiting time for the person doing it.

Balancing the cycle times of each connected process thus becomes very important to ensure efficient and smooth working.

Please see Chapter 25, which deals with Full Man Process, for more details about how to decide which cycle time is best and how to do line balancing.

CHAPTER 19

INCREASING EFFICIENCY

I. DEFINITION OF EFFICIENCY

Man-hours (or machine-hours)
per unit of work

That is it!

Nothing else.

Efficiency is probably the most misunderstood and avoided element of maximising returns and developing people.

I have repeatedly seen that manufacturing organisations tend to treat this topic with caution and with as distanced an approach as possible. It is left to specialists. Basically, once work step times are established by some agreed method, they are not revisited without some kind of investment.

Organisations which provide service or non-physical products and do 'office'-type work often do not see how this applies.

Both types of organisation have units of work, some of which are very standard and some of which are variable.

The definition of efficiency applies equally to both.

In manufacturing, the definition became associated with the combative roles of industrial engineering and the workforce. A history of perceived abuse by management has led the trade unions in these industries to almost innately hate the whole concept, so management, particularly in large and established companies, avoid addressing it directly.

During my apprenticeship in GM's Bedford Truck plant in the UK, I was assigned to the industrial engineering department. 'Time study,' as the shop floor knew it.

The training was based upon the time study engineer doing a stopwatch measurement of process cycle times and then negotiating with the supervisor and trade union representative of the area to get the lowest possible cycle time 'signed off.' Based upon these times, the manning of the processes was calculated and the supervisors had to report the reasons why they exceeded the allowed number of man-hours calculated for the quantity of work. As a new time study engineer, when I walked along the gangway in the cab trim department with my clipboard and stopwatch I would hear a strange 'pinging' noise every now and then. When the first bolt actually hit me, rather than the wall behind me, I realised what the noise was! Time study engineers were universally detested by everyone in the workplace.

We, the time study engineers, made life difficult for both the people and the supervisors. Naturally, the enmity was reciprocated and the whole process became a battle of tricks and wits.

The supervisor would choose the slowest worker to take part in the study. The unions would stringently control the pace of movement. The time study person would judge how honest the cycle times were that had been measured and find ways to 'adjust' them down.

This is one of the factors which made automation of generic cycle times based upon fixed time allowances for each type of movement the more attractive and simpler way forward for many organisations. 'People make problems.'

The difference between process efficiency as applied by TPS and that applied by other traditional organisations is not the tools, they are the same, it is who uses them and the 'perceived ethics' of application. In TPS, time and motion and method study is owned by the people doing the work.

II. TEAMWORK – THE FOUNDATION

Organising a workforce into teams is nothing new.

Giving teams responsibility for organising their own work

methods and efficiency is less universal. Especially where the workload varies over time and periodic rebalancing processes between individuals and teams is necessary to maintain efficiency.

Even further, expecting the teams to improve the efficiency of their own processes is relatively rare.

As discussed earlier in the book, the minimum requirement for this level of engagement is confidence amongst the 'permanent' workforce that their personal job security is an important priority of the organisation which employs them.

Employing a team leader for each team with sufficient time off-process to enable these things is counter-intuitive from a purely headcount point of view, but is essential for success.

I remember, during a visit to one large Toyota plant in Japan, the management excitedly explaining to me that they had made dramatic improvement in efficiency by removing the team leader role.

Having spent the previous 24 years in a non-Toyota environment, the importance of the team leader role was obvious to me.

To the people in the plant, who grew up inside the organisation, which of the many elements that made up Toyota's system were actually vital and which were 'just one way of doing things' was less obvious.

I was frankly shocked and raised the issue, during a discussion with the global head of production, later in the same Japan trip.

"I think they are throwing the baby out with the bathwater!" I remember saying with some passion.

He said, "You are exactly right Carl san."

"So why have they been allowed to do it?"

He smiled at me and said, "How else will they learn this lesson for themselves? They will not hurt anyone or the business in any permanent way by doing what they have done and they are trying to do a good thing. They are good people, give them time."

Six months later, when the effects of removing the team leaders began to become visible in many negative ways, they reversed their previous decision.

The team leader takes the role of an older sibling in a family.

They train the other team members, listen to and advise them, ensure they are safe and operating in a way which will secure their future. The team leader also teaches the team members how to measure the element time and cycle time of the processes and how to identify and eliminate the 7 wastes.

Finally, the team leader teaches them how to make and use the Process Memory Documents.

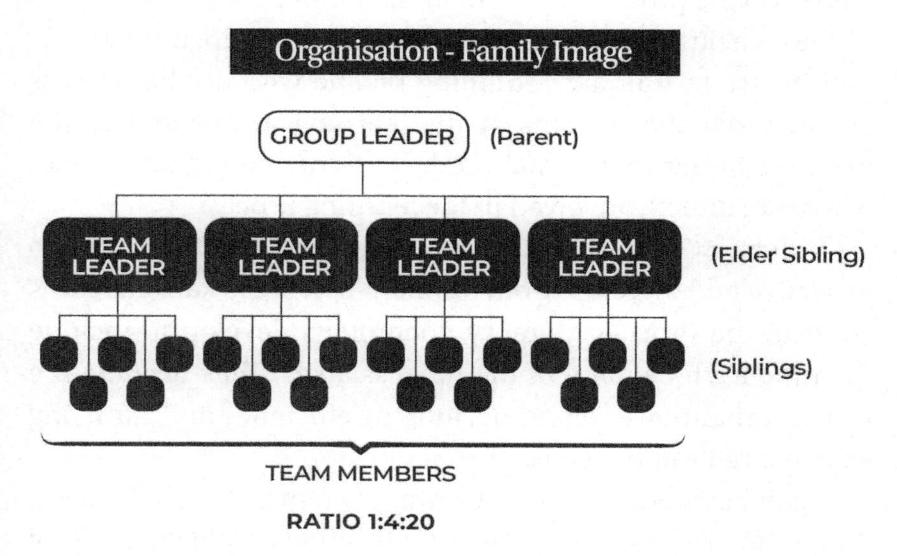

Like a family, the ideal ratio of leaders to team members and group leaders to team leaders is 1:5. This allows each level to fully support the level below in all the ways required. In the diagram above, the number of team leaders to each group leader is shown as 1:4. This ratio of 1:4:20 has been found to work very well in Toyota plants, although not theoretically ideal in terms of man-hours per unit.

III. PROCESS MEMORY – THE BASELINE

Process Memory documents form the basis of every aspect of efficiency and kaizen.

In Section One of the book, we explained the need for Process Memory in capturing the learning that our people get from Practical Problem-Solving.

From a development point of view, the Process Memory documents not only capture the current best method of working, but also enable that knowledge to be used by everyone who does the process now and in the future.

From a business progress point of view, the documentation and its use in training/retraining people who do the process ensures that the benefits of the learning are passed to the business rather than remain only with the individual or team who were directly involved in the learning process.

In Section Two of the book, we are moving from Stabilising to Proactive and therefore from problem-solving to kaizen. In this context, the Process Memory documents develop to include the time each element of the process takes. They become the basis for manpower planning, judging efficiency and clarifying kaizen targets and results.

Again, ownership of the documents remains with the team doing the process. (In mature organisations the ownership of the documentation for any particular process is often with one of the team members.)

The owners take the times for their work. Originally, it was a laborious task using stopwatches and sketches and relied heavily upon skills acquired by repeated practice. The universal availability of simple video equipment, which shows the elapsed time in tenths of seconds, has made this task much easier and the accuracy more reliable.

The following two simple examples of a work step sheet and a job element sheet also show how the team members are taught to break the work down into elements which can be segregated into value-added and non-value-added elements.

The definition of value added is any work which directly adds customer value to the product. Walking, getting and checking elements of the example are clearly non-value-added. With experience, the team members will also study how far they have to physically reach their arms in order to carry out the actual assembly and tightening elements.

All of these non-value-added elements are clear opportunities for kaizen by moving the parts and process as close together as possible. The cycle time is reduced logically and practically by the staff members without increasing the pace of work.

The kaizened-out non-value-added work can then be replaced with value added within the original cycle time.

Work Step Sheet

Authorised by Group Leader: (1st Level of Management) ....
Owner/Author: Team Leader (or Team Member) ....
Group AAAAAAAA Team BBBBBBB
Revision: 1 Date 01/02/03

Process Name: Assembling Stuff

No.	Work Step	Time (secs)
1	Check Manifest to confirm variant	2,0
2	Assemble part 2 to part 1	20,0
3	Assemble part 3 to part 1	19,0
4	Check Correct Assembly	5,0
5	Pass to next Process	4,0
	Total Process Cycle Time	**50,0**

Job Element Sheet

Authorised by Group Leader: (1st Level of Management) ....
Owner/Author: Team Leader (or Team Member) ....
Group AAAAAAAA Team BBBBBBB
Revision: 1 Date 01/02/03

Process Name: Assembling Stuff
WORK STEP 2: ASSEMBLE PART 2 TO PART 1

No.	Job Element	Time (secs)
1	Walk to flow rack	0,5
2	Pick up part 2 according to manifest	1,0
3	Walk to part 1	0,5
4	Locate part 2 on part 1	2,5
5	Get 4 fasteners from box	3,0
6	Loosely assemble 4 fasteners	5,5
7	Get gun	1,0
8	Tightne fasteners	5,0
9	Replace gun	1,0
	Total Work Step Cycle Time	**20,0**

CHAPTER 20

THE 7 WASTES

or

What every employee needs to know

THE 7 WASTES

I. WHAT ARE THEY?

In Chapter 16 we discussed overburden (Muri) and unevenness (Mura). The two types of loss which top management awareness and policy decisions can influence greatly.

There is a third category used by Toyota, Muda, which translates simply as 'Waste', but which breaks down into 7 subcategories.

Any act which does not directly add value to the product is waste. Some wastes are unavoidable. It is necessary to pick up a document to read it, that is necessary, but how far away the document is initially located can be adjusted. Even unavoidable waste can be reduced.

All other waste should be eliminated completely as soon as possible.

In the same way the Muri and Mura are important and for top management to consider, so Muda is helpful for all members of an organisation to be able to identify. They lend focus and structure to kaizen.

The 7 subcategories are:

1. Defects
2. Inventory
3. Transportation
4. Motion
5. Waiting
6. Overproduction
7. Overprocessing

1.DEFECTS

A. DEFINITION

In Section One, we discussed the impact of work which does not meet the customer's standard.

This definition expands the concept of customer from the customer of the finished product to include each process from start to finish of the preparation of the product.

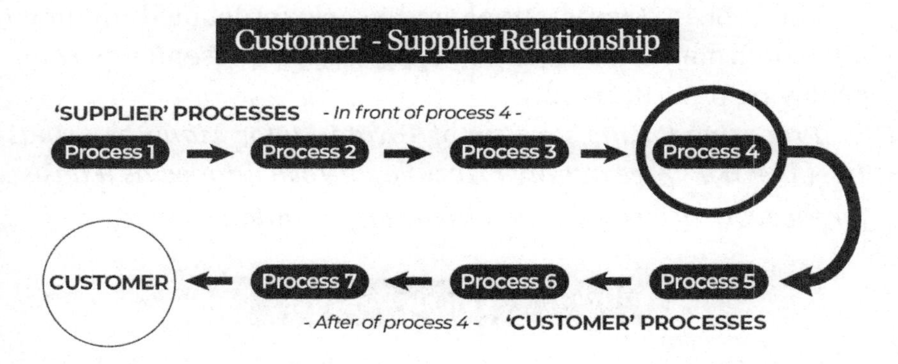

Each process is the customer of each process before it in the preparation sequence. Each process is the supplier of each process after it in the preparation sequence.

For example, the immediate supervisor of Process 4 in the illustration has the responsibility to feed back any problems to the process from which it originates and to follow up for immediate containment and root cause countermeasure.

Likewise, Process 4 owes guaranteed quality and an immediate response to problems for all subsequent processes.

Top management's role in this is to make this direct ownership of quality by each process our minimum expectation and to make a point of positively confirming it when it is relevant.

B. BUILT-IN QUALITY

Quality is the result of correct input and correct process.

The elements of the process, their sequence and how each element is carried out are vital to achieve it.

Also, each process and element needs to have a clear definition of what is good quality and what is no good.

Finally, each element of the process must be able to confirm whether the required quality has been achieved each time.

The Process Memory tool, and its use in detailed training and confirmation of correct activity, plays an essential part in achieving Built-In Quality.

Preparing for the start up of Toyota Motor Manufacturing UK (TMUK), three quality principles were developed as a basis for the work of every division in the organisation.

The Three Quality Principles

1. CUSTOMER EXPECTATIONS DETERMINE THE QUALITY

1.1 The quality level is based upon the expectations of the customer, not on our own experiences or circumstances.

1.2 We always seek to delight the customer, by exceeding the quality level required.

2. HIGH QUALITY IS "BUILT-IN" AT EVERY STAGE.

2.1 Standardised work is used to provide consistent high quality.

2.2 We always watch for irregularities and never pass on poor quality to the next stage.

2.3 We perform Root Cause Countermeasures to prevent problems recurring and continually search for a better way.

3. QUALITY IS CONTINUALLY IMPROVED.

3.1 The quality target is reviewed, in a timely fashion, in order to continue to reflect the rising expectations of our customers.

3.2 We strive to achieve the revised Quality Target, using creativity and teamwork, and working closely with our suppliers.

A very clear and measurable grasp of the quality standard expected by the customer was the starting point. The expected standard was a baseline which should never be breached. Exceeding the customer's expectations was striven for by everyone, but there was an awareness that demanding perfection, i.e. unnecessarily high quality from our 'suppliers', sometimes had a big impact on costs. Overquality is as big a waste as defects. Making the correct standard very clearly defined was the business responsibility of the quality assurance engineers.

It is essential to recognise that we are not automatons but humans with all the complexities and distractions that brings. Finding simple and effective methods to prevent errors being made because of a momentary lapse is important.

These methods are called Poka Yoke (error proofing) in Toyota. Teams are encouraged to develop those which can be made by their own team or with the help of the local process/quality/maintenance engineer.

2. INVENTORY

The impact of excess inventory has been covered in Chapter 17.

However, it is also important to recognise that the benefits of operating with the lowest possible lot size and smallest packaging far outweigh any increase in packaging or transport costs.

Geographic locations made frequent deliveries from any one supplier in isolation impractical for Toyota in Europe and North America, but making 'milk run' collections from several suppliers in the same area made the principle workable.

The milk-run method of logistics made reusable packaging and dunnage, to protect the parts, possible which also helped costs and environmental impact.

3. TRANSPORTATION

Transportation was covered in Chapter 18.

Any change of location of parts or units in progress is classed as transport, whether it is internal or external.

The location of suppliers, equipment, processes all materially affect the amount of transportation waste.

Storage automatically adds to the number of times anything is handled.

4. MOTION

Motion is any movement of the body.

For the members working in genba (the 'shop floor'), motion is the most visible and practical waste to address beneficially.

Walking motion is usually the highest level of impact to process efficiency and reducing the number of steps any process requires to complete is usually the first thing the staff members can recognise and address. Moving equipment closer together and nearer to the point of where the value-added work is done can reduce cycle time dramatically.

Next are turning the body and arm movements. More experienced staff members can reduce process cycle times by carefully relocating equipment and parts closet to the value-added work point and ensuring their orientation reduces the need for turning the body or bending/stretching.

Very experienced members of staff working with processes which have already reached a high level of efficiency go further and study head movement and even the need to look to locate parts.

5. WAITING

Any time between one process or job element flowing smoothly into the subsequent one is classed as waiting.

It is the most tragic of all wastes because it not only reduces efficiency but, more importantly, also shows great disrespect to the people doing the work. (Their time is unimportant.)

Some waiting is obvious to see, for example when a breakdown happens, parts are delayed or a key person does not turn up to a meeting on time.

Harder to identify, but often much greater in cumulative effect, are the waiting resulting from not fully utilising the available cycle time during process design/balancing or from disturbances which interfere with smooth process flow.

6. OVERPRODUCTION

"An idle machine or person is a waste of money," my old boss used to say. "Keep them moving son, you know their cost per part is less for every additional part they make. Run them as fast as you can."

This sage advice stayed with me for the 23 and a half years I worked for General Motors.

So I did, and, as a result, we had many more of several parts than we could use. No two machines produced at exactly the same speed, and the production plan was based upon theoretical capacities, so we needed an army of stock controllers to keep track of what we had versus what we needed of each part. They were in another department, which wasn't subject to efficiency measurement, and they were 'indirect' labour.

Our production department's efficiency measure of man-hours per unit produced was always very good at each section and area. Somehow, we never looked at the number from the point of view of what actually went to the customer.

When customer demand was slow, we filled every square metre of floor space and racking with surplus parts. Keeping them organised and ensuring that each engineering change was introduced only after the parts made to the previous standard had been used up was a nightmare.

During my first week in Toyota, I was introduced to the concept of the 'pull' system of production management.

As one small box of parts is started to be used by a process, a signal is sent to the previous process to make another box of parts to replace them. No signal, no production.

KANBAN Replenishment card

YOUR LOGO
KANBAN REPLENISHMENT CARD
Part Number: XXXX
Description: XXXX
Picture of part
Order Qty: XXXX
U/M: XXXX
Card 1 of: XXXX
Container: XXXX
Pull from: XXXX
Supplier: XXXX
Pull to: XXXX
Consuming Operation: XXXX
CARD ID & BARCODE

The signal is transmitted manually by an order (kanban) card which the supplying process places with the box of parts and which is removed by the user as the first part is taken out of the box. The cards are sent back to the supplying process very frequently.

In this way only what is needed by the customer is made when it is needed. Production is synchronised with the customer's need.

7. OVERPROCESSING

This was partly covered when we were discussing quality. Making products to a higher specification than the customer needs is a very clear waste.

Putting an extra element in a process 'just to be sure' is also overprocessing. (For example, when a part is pressed home in an assembly and the machine is set to press a second time in case the part was not completely pressed home the first time.)

Designing the manual or machine process so that a good result is guaranteed just by doing the process correctly avoids such waste.

The finish machining cut which is too fine or the heat treatment cycle which takes the part to a higher temperature than necessary or 'soaks' the part too long are other examples.

A process confirming the quality from a previous process is also overprocessing. The previous process should confirm before passing the work on.

Learning to see the 7 wastes when they are present in any process or system comes only from practice. Selecting a bottleneck process and consciously observing and studying it for each waste is a good method of combining business priority with development.

BOTH WHEELS IN BALANCE

In Toyota, this is called Jishuken. An area or line which is a business priority is selected for improvement. The related team leaders and engineer/specialists will first confirm that the line is performing to current standards. The Jishuken team will often be made up of management, engineers, specialists, group leaders and team leaders from other areas for a 'fresh eyes' viewpoint, plus the local first line supervisor and some of the local team leaders. The processes are studied for the 7 wastes and many kaizen are proposed and simulated during a 1 or 2-week intensive assignment. The local teams and their engineers/ specialists are then supported during the following 3 to 5 weeks to implement the improvements. The line is then rebalanced to realise the business benefits. Alternatively, in more mature areas, the line will be rebalanced immediately and the staff members that have been released by the kaizen will stay to support until the Jishuken ideas have been successfully implemented.

The Jishuken members from outside the line are selected from the areas which are the next priority. They can then lead the Jishuken in their own areas upon their return.

CHAPTER 21

SMOOTHNESS

or

The smoothest process is always the lowest cost process

WHAT IS SMOOTHNESS?

An understandable way to describe smoothness is to use the analogy of the daily journey to work.

Most of us leave home and either drive, cycle or walk to work.

On a normal day, we get in the car, for example, and head off on the standard route.

Most days, we arrive at work and, if asked what happened on the journey, would be unable to remember much detail. We would just say we had had a good journey.

We drove in a kind of mental 'autopilot' mode, safely and smoothly. Time passed quickly, and we probably thought about many other things than driving whilst we were on the way.

If something abnormal happens, like a cyclist suddenly swerving in our path, we are immediately back in the present and conscious of everything happening around us.

If every set of lights on the journey are red, and we are forced to remain focused on each one until they turn green, we would say we had a terrible journey. Similarly for heavy traffic situations and so on.

The smooth process is similar to the good journey to work. The member of staff doing the process can 'get into the groove' and perform the tasks without having to focus every second of the day. Muscle memory, which includes the brain 'muscle', combined with no abnormalities make the process run smoothly. At the end of the day the staff member is still mentally fresh and has had a good day at work. The safety, quality and efficiency of the work are secure.

If an abnormal situation occurs, the staff member immediately snaps back to full focus.

In Toyota, seeing something unusual or abnormal prompts the line member to immediately 'pull the Andon' to call the team leader. This allows the member of staff doing the process to continue with their standard process and the team leader to take care of the abnormality.

When the day is full of abnormalities, the staff member becomes mentally and often physically exhausted and frustrated.

Each interruption brings the risk of a mistake being made, especially when it happens during the process cycle. It leaves the member of staff trying to recall, "Where was I in the process?"

An activity which happens quickly and smoothly when using 'muscle memory' is much more difficult when it has to be done with full focus of the conscious brain. (Shaving is a good example of this.)

Normal process speed and, therefore, efficiency cannot be maintained.

Each member of management and each team in Toyota work hard to eliminate as many of the abnormalities as possible.

Every year, as head of a Toyota plant, I would have to sign 300 to 500 Christmas cards to related businesses and other organisations. I would set a fun challenge each year to complete the task in less time, using TPS principles.

So one staff member would be selecting and positioning each card in front of me to sign. I would sign and pass the card to another member of staff who would put the card ready for the next person.

When things went smoothly my signatures were always good.

When an interruption happened, I would find myself having to sign with my conscious mind. The quality of those signatures was not so good. (Try writing your signature with your mind fully engaged.) Signatures are a classic example of 'muscle memory' activity.

By the way, 78 cards per minute was the record.

Out of interest, the necessary non-value-added elements were 70% of the process, regardless of who did them. Oh, and I broke a cardinal rule of TPS by working at a pace which was not sustainable comfortably all day. (It was just a bit of fun.)

Achieving smoothness from the individual staff member's viewpoint, i.e. to fully establish muscle memory, takes between 800 and 900 cycles of the process for the average person.

By 350 cycles, the staff member can normally maintain consistent performance at the correct pace with little or no support, but it is hard work for them.

CHAPTER 22

4S

or

A base for kaizen to achieve engagement, ownership, efficiency and development in the workplace

DEFINITION

The term 4S is derived from the 4 Japanese words used by Toyota to describe the activity of creating a safe, efficient and attractive workplace.

Out of interest, the four words are Seiri, Seiso, Seiton and Seiketsu.

These represent the 4 elements of the activity and, although they do not translate exactly, the elements, or steps, of 4S can best be described in English as follows:

1. Only items of immediate use should be in the workplace. Other items should be removed.
2. A clearly marked location for every item in the workplace and the items always in their marked location.
3. Everything in the workplace maintained ready for immediate use.
4. A clean, bright and attractive workplace.

PURPOSE

As with everything in the management system, the 4S discipline has many direct and indirect benefits:

1. It introduces the concept and importance of standardisation. The team and, if the area is shared, all of the user teams or groups discuss and reach consensus about which items are needed and where is their best location. Decision criteria are safety, convenience, efficiency and appearance.
2. The importance of being able to find everything

immediately and it being ready to use becomes obvious. The area runs smoothly.

3. Missing or incorrectly placed items are easily noticeable as is the correct quantity of each item needed for smooth working.
4. The interdependency of all team members adhering to the standards in order to maintain a good condition becomes obvious.
5. The need for clear and fair planning and responsibilities to achieve and maintain cleanliness.
6. The team members have direct input regarding what is considered a bright and attractive workplace. They can make it their personal area by the layout they choose and also the things they choose for decoration, display, etc.
7. The team members' pride in their workplace is a natural outcome of 4S activity.

4S quickly forms the foundation of many of the basic disciplines of TPS, and especially Kaizen, in a way which enables the team and group leaders to be able to coach and support excellence through simple, daily examples.

The concept and practice apply to all workplaces in all types of organisation. The key factor is the involvement of all of the related staff members in the decisions and maintenance of the condition.

The discipline quickly translates to the way each individual thinks and behaves in other aspects of work and even life.

For instance, 4S is frequently used in Toyota as a general term to mean sorting and sifting the information or topics of any subject in order to make it manageable and easy to communicate and improve. For example:

"Would it be helpful to 4S this marketing data to know where the biggest opportunities are?"

When we introduced the practice in TMUK, we decided to roll it out plant wide in four steps, one step per month.

Step one was called "NEED/NO NEED" and the staff members got rid of all the duplicated and accumulated stuff in their rest areas. The unnecessary things were returned to the central stores. The store management people complained about not having enough room for it all! Some things, like stationery did not need to be ordered by the plant for quite a few weeks.

Step two was called "A PLACE FOR EVERYTHING AND EVERYTHING IN ITS PLACE".

The third step was "READY TO USE". It shocked many of the staff members how many of the simple things made such a difference to their smoothness of getting things done. Equipment was kept on shadow boards and maintenance particularly got great benefit from them.

Finally, we had the: "CLEAN, BRIGHT AND ATTRACTIVE" step. I think, by an accumulation of each group's efforts, we must have relamped half the plant, but it was worth every penny.

The managers wanted to recognise their people's great work, and so we made first, second and third place rosettes for the best rest areas, and the plant president came down to each shop and office, one at a time, to tour and to have the first place group present what they had done to him themselves.

The second place group presented to the vice presidents and the third place groups to the directors.

The communication that happened between the group leaders and their people and with each other on this common 'mission' was more than just a side benefit.

Each shift took ownership of leaving their area for the next shift as they would wish to find it.

We, as the management team, had, of course, to serve as examples of the expected standard. It is not exaggerating to say it taught us quite a bit too.

Before doing the activity, we would spend quite some time in levelling up the plant's appearance to receive VIP visitors.

Within 12 months, the need for any levelling up had gone. Everyone was happy that any visitor could walk in unannounced at any time and we would be proud to show them around.

Identifying and marking a place for everything makes visual management easy for the team and also for management. Any abnormality can be seen just by walking past and taking notice.

It also helps with sharing good ideas between teams and groups, as everyone can see each other's ideas.

Incidentally, the sharing of good ideas between teams, groups, departments, plants and even companies is another well-established Toyota principle. It is called Yokoten.

CHAPTER 23

SEPARATING NORMAL FROM ABNORMAL

or

The importance of not mixing up standard situations with non-standard situations

WHAT *ARE* YOU TALKING ABOUT CARL?

Strangely enough, this was something that was never clearly explained within my years in management but is such an important concept and tool that I need to explain it here.

When our operations are running normally, at whatever level of smoothness and efficiency that currently is reality, it means that many things are operating, to some extent, in a standard way.

People know what to do, when and how. This is the cumulative result of people's systems, experience, training and practice.

Whether we judge it to be a 'good' condition doesn't really matter. The point is that a lot of effort and struggles have paved the way to reach the current status.

This is very precious. It was a big investment.

When something abnormal happens that threatens the quality of the output or performance of our organisation, it is our job as management to deal with the situation as quickly and efficiently as possible.

It is a natural reaction to quickly change the way things are done to accommodate and manage the threat. For example, at the micro level, we add a couple of elements to the process of the current operators, or add an additional check to the inspection member's work.

Like all of the concepts we discuss in this book, this applies at the macro as well as the micro levels.

For example, in the case of the coronavirus, we witnessed whole nations changing all of the normal things. Work stopped, travel stopped, education stopped. The impact of the virus itself will be significant, but the impact of stopping all of the 'standard' systems and practices will make that pale into insignificance.

The UK government created 4000-bed capacity Nightingale hospitals at five locations across the country. If these facilities had been used to handle all coronavirus cases they would have served a very useful purpose. The standard hospitals would have been able to continue normal services to a much higher degree. Patients would also have been more confident that they were not risking exposure to the virus by being hospitalised. The large secondary impact caused by cessation of treatment for other diseases and illnesses would have been avoided to a greater extent.

In this case, the concept of separating the treatment of the virus from other 'standard' treatments was made possible, but, unfortunately not utilised.

(I am in no way saying that the virus should have been left to take its natural course regardless of the consequences. There were many effective ways of protecting from transmission of the virus which would have controlled the speed of its progress.)

By immediately putting containment for the problem in place, we protect the standard operations and avoid all the secondary risks that disruption of them brings.

Containment means additional resources and requires a high level of management focus to maintain effectively.

It is always worthwhile, no matter how expensive or difficult.

In addition to protecting the standard processes already in place, and therefore the current level of performance, it also sends a very clear message to the whole organisation about how important the standards really are.

Getting any organisation to realise just how vital maintaining standards is has proved to be one of the most difficult challenges management face.

Every opportunity should be taken to clearly 'walk the walk' as opposed to just 'talk the talk'.

This gives everyone the confidence to do what is best, even when management is not immediately available.

The cost of the containment is recovered when the team, in which the issue was identified, find the root cause and permanent countermeasure for the issue. (Of course with as much support as they need, without removing their ownership.)

One example, of not disturbing the standard process, is when the Toyota team member pulls the Andon. The line does not stop immediately. It continues to move as normal until the end of the normal process cycle time. This is so that the rest of the members on the line can finish their process normally and can start the next process at the beginning as they would at the start of the shift or after a break.

Interrupting them in mid-cycle is often more risky than the original issue for which the Andon was pulled.

Another example is the way the members of a team or group are kept together as a unit as a high management priority.

In General Motors plants, there would be a morning 'labour market'. The heads of each department would gather in the production director's office and declare the attendance level within their responsible area. Then a debate would follow which decided how much 'labour' would be transferred between departments for that day. The importance of the role of each individual was simply not recognised. "Any pair of hands will do."

In Toyota, the team leader steps in to cover any absence within their team and, if needed, the group leader would step into a team leader or team member's role for that shift. Each individual's skill and experience in their role was highly valued and protected. Members of staff knew they were individually important.

Remember: protect the standard situation at all costs and under all circumstances.

CHAPTER 24

MUTUAL TRUST AND RESPECT

I. MUTUAL TRUST

Mutual trust in an organisation is not a theoretical or emotional concept.

It is a very practical and vital characteristic of any powerful and sustained organisation.

It is based upon several elements:

1. Common values.
2. Factual and logical thinking.
3. Commitments defined and honoured.
4. Openness and visualisation.
5. Consensus.

1. COMMON VALUES

In several places throughout this book, we have discussed the need for common priorities and common policies being vital to enable all members of an organisation to be able to confidently take decisions in their workplace. Especially when the decision taken may not be the most financially expedient option available.

Communication of these values to all employees, and to all new employees during new employee induction, is essential.

One example is when an organisation says it prioritises employee safety above everything else and has a clear policy that work will stop immediately, and correct the situation, rather than continue in a risky or unsafe manner.

It is easy to understand the priority and policy.

Only when all decisions, which have been to stop the process even though they costs money and risk volume loss, are applauded and openly appreciated by the management team can the organisation know that they have common safety values.

Naturally, it is management's role to respond as quickly as possible where a problem has been highlighted.

Job security, or the lack of it, is the common value which results in the most visible and immediate resistance for kaizen. Where an organisation sees labour as an expense rather than an investment job security is small. Redundancy and lay-offs are the first steps of cost reduction in difficult times. After all, labour is the most impactful and flexible cost for such organisations.

People do know that no job is 100% secure. The nature of business has a natural fluctuation.

Mutual trust begins when people are seen as a developing and maturing investment. Surplus people are utilised to accelerate improvement, so the organisation can come back fitter and stronger when circumstances improve or new business is won because of improved competitiveness.

Everyone understands that when retaining employees becomes a direct threat to the survival of the organisation reduction of employees must be considered.

2. FACTUAL AND LOGICAL THINKING

Isn't it every manager's dream to be able to delegate whole issues to subordinates with full confidence that they will take care of them completely and efficiently?

All employees knowing the company's values is very helpful in achieving this, but it isn't enough.

The employees need to be able to handle the issue correctly.

When employees gather the true facts of a situation and logically reach a conclusion about which actions to take, management confidence in them grows.

When top management insist upon and coach the use of facts and logic in all situations, the organisation follows.

It is a tough discipline, which initially will seem to take a long time to reach decisions, but the benefits in speed and effectiveness will continue to grow as the skill of using facts and logic grow within the organisation.

Hearing such phrases as "I know what this is", "We had this before and I know what to do", "I think it is this", "In my opinion it is..." should act as immediate warnings for the senior person present to step in and insist upon following only the facts and logic to find out the real issue.

Go and See is crucial in this.

Insisting upon the facts and logic being explained using a documented form, such as Practical Problem-Solving or A3 format, helps with both confirmation and coaching.

The confirmation of each step of the logic used in the analysis can be as simple as confirming that there is evidence for each conclusion made. Carefully checking that no conclusions are based upon assumption or experience is very effective.

Never allowing shortcuts to be taken is difficult at first, especially where previous leaders have focused only upon the speed of 'doing something'.

The benefits are more than worth every ounce of the top management effort required.

3. COMMITMENTS DEFINED AND HONOURED

How many times do you hear that unexpected issues arose and the estimated time or cost of delivery of an agreed objective has to be increased?

How many times do you hear this at, or after, the point at

which the objective should have been achieved?

Or you hear that the objective has been achieved, but when you confirm the actual achievement there is a gap between what has been delivered and your expectation?

Suddenly, the budget and manpower allocation plans so carefully made are thrown into disarray. People, equipment or money which were planned to be used on the next assignment are needed to complete the current one.

At this point, the process moves out of management control and into the realms of 'doing our best'. From this point, management are no longer able to support or confirm progress in any concrete or practical way.

Any of this remind you of previous or current experiences?

It is not uncommon to observe such situations.

DEFINED COMMITMENT

Time taken to confirm a clear and common understanding of the expectations of an assignment is small, but it is often skipped because of assumption or that the requirement is 'common sense'.

(By the way, doesn't 'common sense' seem to be the rarest commodity in the known universe?)

Any expectation which cannot be numerically measured and time-bound is both risky and unfair. People will spend their precious time and effort to try to meet the expectation. Their own ability to be able to judge progress and success with confidence is a precondition of real success. To finish, after much effort, and be told "That is not what I expected" is truly soul-destroying.

By discussion and clarification, any expectation can be defined in such a way as to be measurable.

If it cannot, then the expectation is not sufficiently understood by anybody involved and best dropped until it is.

A mutually agreed and clearly measurable expectation is the start of any assignment.

HONOURED COMMITMENT

Defining an expectation with clear, time-bound and measurable parameters is often unconsciously avoided by everyone involved because once it is done there is no room to manoeuvre. It seems a very strict and demanding way to manage.

In isolation, it is.

(In fact, where the management demands only results and has no interest in the process used to deliver, it is actually dangerous for the people assigned, as it causes them maximum stress and minimum motivation.) That is why the Andon is so important.

THE ANDON

In organisations which operate under the ethics and practice of the 'Andon' (described in an earlier chapter) it is not so.

The whole organisation appreciates the importance of delivering on time and on target and supports its achievement. If failure happens, it is only after everyone who could help has done all they can to prevent it. This is right up to the president of the company, if necessary. Where the objective cannot be achieved, even at this level, the objective-setting method clearly has a problem or circumstances changed a lot.

When success is achieved, it is extremely important to remember that the Andon was 'pulled' in a timely manner by the person who owned the objective. The whole credit goes to them. Their unselfish act of 'pulling the Andon' prevented the organisation from failing an objective.

The importance of 'management control' being maintained is not a commonly understood priority. The term 'Being in management control' means being able to do what is planned, when it is planned and with the correct resources.

If, despite everyone's best efforts, an activity is not following its plan, the plan must be immediately adjusted to come back into control.

Management control requires concrete planning with interim milestones well defined and well confirmed. The milestones help everyone to understand if progress is in line with the plan in time to overcome any risk of failure. The ability to do this well is one of the things developed and coached using openness and visualisation.

4. OPENNESS AND VISUALISATION

OPENNESS

Top management set the tone of the whole organisation. Working hard to control one's personal response to information and always ensuring that a positive atmosphere is maintained is not easy, or natural, for many people.

Sometimes, there would be a tangible period of silence when the person presenting a topic to me would say or show something which was clearly so far away from the truth, or showed such a lack of understanding of the necessary tools, that I needed a few moments to think carefully how to respond in such a way so as to make the progress of the meeting positive.

On one occasion, a team member explained to me her conclusions from the analysis she had done to find the cause of a particular problem in the process. The data she was presenting and her conclusions simply were not compatible. It was blatantly obvious without any need for special skill or knowledge. It simply could not be true. My frustration was very high, but to show it would have been a disaster. The team member had worked hard to prepare her presentation. Because she was presenting to the president of the company, her management team owed her the support of confirming the presentation before inviting me to come and see it.

So there were several possibilities. The management team between the staff member and me had not done their duty of support and care, or, sadly, they also did not see such an obvious issue when they confirmed the findings.

After a few seconds of silent consideration, I was able to thank the staff member for her hard work and to gently ask her and her management team to check the logic again, because I could not quite follow the connections between the data and the conclusion.

After the meeting, her general manager and I discussed what had happened and why there was a disconnection between the facts and the conclusion.

He had indeed confirmed the presentation in advance, and the staff member's presentation had been quite different. She had followed the data and reached a logical conclusion. However, the general manager had overheard a previous discussion between me and another manager in which he understood that I thought that one particular cause was obvious. He had adjusted the original presentation so that it came to the conclusion he thought I preferred. He wanted to please his president.

I apologised to him for allowing a situation in which 'pleasing the boss' was more important than following the data to the logical conclusion and assured him that I would never challenge any conclusion that could be demonstrated to be based on the full facts and sound logic.

We can influence the work of our subordinates without even realising it. A casual comment about which option seems best at first glance, or even a furrowing of the eyebrows when something is said in a meeting, can send strong signals to the team.

Accepting and supporting a conclusion which is surprising or even, at first glance, strange, if it is based upon solid facts and sound logic also sends strong positive signals.

Underestimating one's unconscious power as a senior member of management is quite common. We just can't believe our influence can be so strong. But it truly is.

When presenting the half-yearly or annual performance and issues of my plant to the senior vice presidents of Toyota, in Toyota City in Japan or during their visits to us, or even talking with general managers in the plants, they would always carefully maintain a neutral expression until the end of the presentation. It was very strange for me, so I asked why. They explained that unconscious influence hindered their people's development and power and, at their level, the results of that influence could be dangerous to the organisation.

As one said to me, "Carl san, when your people are investigating any issue, you must never give an opinion. Firstly, you will be telling them that opinions are OK and there is no need for facts and analysis. Secondly, opinion carries more weight the higher the person is in the organisation. You are company president, your opinion is the same as facts for everyone else. When joining subordinates in any meeting it is essential that their voice is heard, not yours, until they have finished. Of course, if you have new information about the issue or an understanding of wider implications because of your position, you should share that in your feedback."

In our cultures, it is quite unnerving if the boss shows no reaction when we are presenting. For us, at least some positive reactions to the correct or exceptional parts of our work are very welcome and encouraging as the presentation progresses.

BAD NEWS FIRST AND ALWAYS

The first time a subordinate sees a negative reaction to bad news is the last time they will bring any. Problems will remain hidden until they make themselves visible in the results.

On the other hand, a sincere 'thank you' and confirmation that enough support is being given to help them overcome the problem will ensure problems are raised in good time.

VISUALISATION

In Section One of the book, we talked about making performance visible. We also talked about the importance of visualising and sharing the steps taken to solve prioritised problems.

The way the visualisation helps teamwork and coaching was also explained.

Similarly, there is enormous benefit in visualising and sharing the planning to meet the organisation's business objectives.

Simply giving targets and monitoring results versus each target will not create an open or powerful organisation.

The most powerful tool for visually promoting both the achievement of business objectives or projects and for creating opportunities for employee development and coaching is the obeya.

(When searching for the word obeya online, it is sometimes

spelled oobeya, where the oo is pronounced as ohh.)

Please see the chapter on obeya.

All good visualisation makes reality crystal clear for all involved. Once again, it is the reaction of management to what the visualisation is showing that promotes either a good, open and developing, or closed and self-protective, situation in the organisation.

5. CONSENSUS

Every sizeable organisation is divided up into manageable subsections, be they teams, sections, departments, divisions or companies.

The leader of each subsection naturally wants to demonstrate their performance through the results of their area of responsibility.

To make best use of resources, an organisation often needs to prioritise which subsections need to make the most progress for the benefit of the whole, whilst others may need to contain their ambitions.

In other words, some parts of the organisation need to take 'a hit' for the benefit of the whole.

(By no means are all organisations able to effectively prioritise, by the way.)

Did you ever walk out of a decision meeting and hear one of the managers present at the meeting say "I don't agree with that. No way is that going to happen in my area!"? This is a lack of consensus.

For effective prioritisation of resources to be practical in reality, the company's assessment of each leader's performances needs to have teamwork and company-wide vision as important parts of their performance review criteria.

More practically still, when alternative actions or methods are being discussed amongst the management team, there will always be more than one viewpoint in any healthy organisation. (Same elephant, different viewpoint.) If someone has an alternative viewpoint or information which materially affects which is the best decision, it is their obligation to raise it clearly during the discussion.

Debate can never continue endlessly, the organisation must move forward.

During the discussion, as many viewpoints and as much relevant information as possible are welcome. A decision should be taken as soon as all the issues are clear enough to be evaluated.

The decision, once taken, is owned by every member of the management team as their own, whatever it is.

The only exception is where new and important information comes to light after the meeting. Then the decision meeting can be quickly reconvened.

Raising further viewpoints or information, which were known at the time of the meeting but not raised, reflects very badly upon the person who did not step forward at the time.

This discipline is consensus.

Tremendous effort is made by the meeting facilitators to gather all related viewpoints and relevant facts before any consensus meeting in Toyota. (Incidentally, this process is known as the nemawashi stage of decision-making.) The summary of the outcome from meetings are organised logically and circulated to all participants prior to the formal meeting, with a proposed decision. Any important omission from the proposal document can and must be raised at this time.

The decision meeting time is then only as long as is needed for the facilitator to present the related information to the assembled participants and a formal "Yoshi!" ("Let's do it!") to be registered.

New information, not available to anyone prior to the consensus meeting, is welcome and a new consensus meeting called if necessary.

Personal opinions have zero value in this process.

The nemawashi process involves a lot of work for the coordinating division, but the resulting decisions are much higher quality and have much more ownership. The execution speed more than makes up for the time spent reaching consensus.

II. MUTUAL RESPECT

Some organisation's speed of progress is less than optimum, because there is confusion about how the different 'levels' of role fit together.

As a result, enormous sources of energy and power remain untapped.

TYPES OF ROLE

It is always true that some roles have greater levels of responsibility and authority than others and salary usually reflects this.

The confusion arises when some roles are seen as 'doers' and others as 'thinkers'. The terms operator or worker are often seen to apply to the 'doer'-type roles.

The expectations management has of people in such roles is often limited to "Please turn up on time, do what you are told and don't give me any problems".

Such roles are seen as easily interchangeable because they are 'low skilled'. People can be moved freely between roles and even departments at any time without expecting any consequences to performance.

The structure of the organisation, its decisions and the communication methods reflect this understanding.

The people employed in such roles naturally fulfil management's expectations. Absenteeism and sick leave are controlled by enforcement procedures. The first line supervisor is expected to maintain performance by strict traditional discipline.

In such organisations, the idea of 'Built-In Quality,' where no additional inspection is needed to confirm it is a pipe dream. No operator has ownership of the job they are doing. They see themselves as eminently replaceable, because that is what happens.

In order to achieve Built-In Quality, each person must understand the risks and purpose behind each element of their role. Even an assembly line process has many such issues. There is no such thing as a 'simple' process which can be grasped and performed without deep knowledge and much physical practice to achieve the correct method and skills.

The idea that operators or workers can and will work to continuously improve the performance of their roles is even more of a pipe dream in such 'traditional' organisations.

From janitor to president, there are different roles and responsibilities amongst people in any organisation.

Regardless of the role, the professionalism with which it is performed is the key.

It is this professionalism which is respected in the healthy organisation.

When competent in the role, the person who owns/ performs it has the right to real involvement in any decision relating to the method with which their responsibility is carried out. Their pride of ownership creates a self-discipline which is stronger than any level of regimentation can provide.

The term '5S' has become very popular when people talk about management tools to create an efficient and attractive workplace. Seiri, Seiso, Seiton, Seiketsu are the 4S's which Toyota uses. These are covered in a separate chapter.

Someone outside Toyota added a fifth S, Shitsuke, which translates roughly to the English word discipline. This is often interpreted to mean control by regular and frequent checking to make sure standards are adhered to.

In reality, Shitsuke means the person doing the job truly understands which are the critical elements of the process and the reason each one is important, and also, how to judge if the result is correct or not.

In other words, 'self-discipline' based upon knowledge. This knowledge can be shared with good Process Memory documentation, but it is given personal ownership when the member of staff doing the process is involved in the root cause and permanent countermeasure of problems they experience.

Making sure that the members of the organisation have the opportunity and expectation to develop such ownership is one of the concrete demonstrations of respect. Regularly sharing the performance and progress of the organisation is another. This provides all the staff members with a common background to decisions which might otherwise seem strange or even detrimental from an individual viewpoint.

At least twice a year, and up to four times in difficult circumstance, I as president and CEO, and the rest of the board would stand up in front of the whole workforce and explain the business circumstances we were working in, the performance against our Direction Deployment (Hoshins) and our performance versus the standard KPIs.

At least two of the top team's problems and learning points would be explained also.

It took a week to prepare and a whole day to present in front of 2000 people on 3 shifts.

The member of staff's questions were either taken live at the meeting or collected through their supervisors and the questions and answers published to everyone within 3 days.

This common knowledge also allows each person to contribute to 'how' the organisation's objectives can best be achieved within their own area, or even in total.

When management follow the organisation's policies and values without any exceptions, staff members quickly learn respect for their supervision and their management team. If expediency in each individual situation is the main driver, even when it goes against the policies and values, the respect, confidence and even the trust of the staff members can be weakened.

CHAPTER 25

THE FULL MAN PROCESS

or

What does process balancing really mean?

DEFINITION OF FULL PROCESS

A full process is one in which 100% of the staff member's nomral working time is filled with 'standardised' or planned work. This applies to all processes be they shop floor or office.

The concept of the Full Process is counter-intuitive for most people. In a Progressive organisation it is very important.

The term Balanced Processes, by its nature, is misleading.

There are three types of process in any organisation.

TYPE 1

The process has a short cycle time (usually seconds or minutes) and is repetitive in content.

TYPE 2

The process has a short cycle time but is variable in content.

TYPE 3

The process has a long cycle time (hours, days or weeks) and is fixed or variable in content. These are most often line support, maintenance or office work.

In each type of work there is a cycle time, which can vary, and the time is subdivided into job elements, which usually need a fixed time to complete.

The volume of work to be done in any given length of time determines the number of people needed to do the work, or, to put it another way, the length of time each person has available to complete each their process. (Higher volume of work = shorter time available for each cycle, hence more people needed to do the same workload in less time.)

The content of each person's work has to be adjusted, up or down, according to the required volume in any given workday etc.

This is true of all work.

Please excuse this short explanation of the obvious, but the background is necessary.

In Toyota, Takt time is used to allocate resources. Takt time means the clock or calendar time available for work divided by the number of products ordered by the customer to be made during that time.

1. Takt time =
10 products per hour = 60 minutes = 6 minutes per product.
÷ 10 Products

or

2. Takt time =
10 reports per week = 40 hours = 4 hours per report.
÷ 10 reports

If the volume of work increases, for example by 50% then the Takt time will reduce accordingly.

Takt time =
15 products per hour = 60 minutes = 4 minutes per product.
÷15 Products

Manpower calculation
If each product takes 0.5 man-hours to produce then the ideal manpower needed = 30 man-minutes ÷ 6 minutes Takt time = 5 people.

If, in the same example, kaizen reduces the time each product takes to 0.44 man-hours to produce then the ideal manpower needed
= 26,4 man-minutes ÷ 6 minutes Takt time = 4,4 people

Clearly there is not enough work to fully occupy five people, but four people cannot do the process.

In such cases most organisations I have seen divide the work equally between the minimum number of processes. (In this case five.)

This *seems* fair and to be common sense.

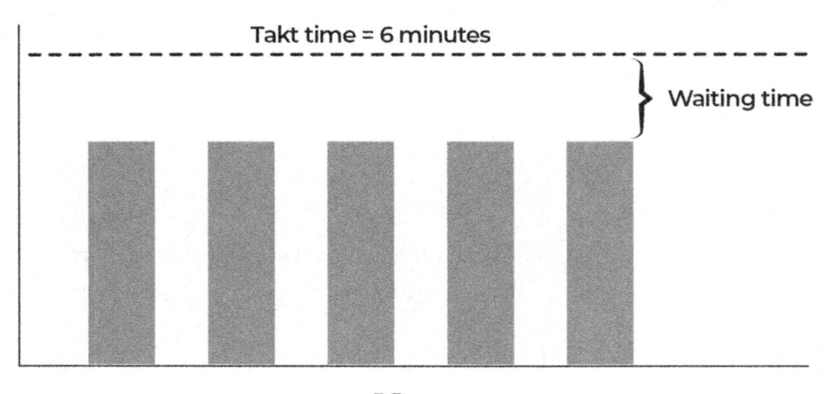

However, in this method, each process has planned waiting time, or waste. (Muda.)

Please see the diagram which follows.

There are several hidden impacts of this 'fair' division of work:

1. The planned waiting time in each process will hide many problems, because the staff member doing the process has time to overcome them. They will soon become 'normal business' and accumulate over time.

2. Theoretically, each member of staff should be seen to stop

and wait for the surplus time without any planned work.

Perhaps you could try that for yourself for a few minutes before continuing please?

Whilst rereading an earlier page of the book, please set a timer to signal after 55 seconds. When the signal sounds please stop for 5 seconds. Just stop and wait until the five seconds are over and then restart the timer for the next 55 seconds and continue reading where you left off, then stop again, etc.

Ten cycles should be more than enough of this exercise.

How did it make you feel? Please take a few seconds to explore your true feelings if your boss asked you to work in this way, all day, every day.

What message is your boss sending you?

You are not so important. It is OK to plan to waste your time.

It is not important that you are able to establish a smooth and comfortable rhythm of work.

You should handle problems by yourself, no matter how frequent or repetitive, because you have 'spare time'.

These are the unconscious signals many employees are sent by their organisation.

Insulting? Denigrating? Impossible to do?

All of those descriptions are apt.

(This is another practical example of the meaning of mutual respect being misunderstood.)

Of course the member of staff doesn't do it!

Within a few cycles, the staff member finds things to do to fill the time; a little double-check of part of the process, an extra little step of moving the parts or data, anything to fill the time and restore self-respect.

All of these things are totally unconscious with the majority of people, both the bosses and the members of staff doing the job, but no less real for that. The culture of the organisation is set.

The 'fill-in' work becomes a standard part of the process very quickly. Wasted work is now 'built-in'.

3. The Process Memory document standard method is now no longer being followed. The efficiency, safety and Built-In Quality are all at risk.

If you subsequently ask the member of staff doing the job if there is any spare time, they will assure you that they are already fully burdened.

Multiply these issues by the number of staff members in the organisation and, suddenly, not only the desired culture is significantly challenged but also efficiency and Built-In Quality.

Recognising these issues, Toyota balances or rebalances each process in a different way.

All processes but one in each team or work group are fully loaded with planned activity.

Title required for this Process Balancing

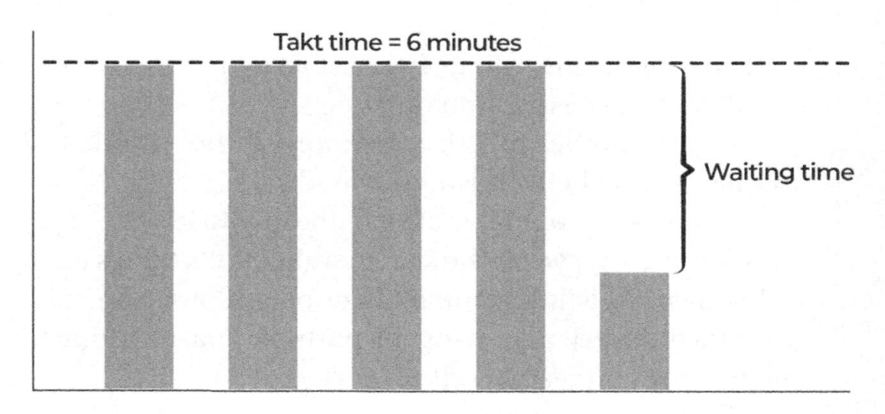

5 Processes

FOUR 'FULL PROCESSES, PLUS ONE CLEARLY UNDERBURDENED

All of the waiting time is placed with one process.

In this way, the staff members can establish smooth working and maintain the work as planned in the Process Memory document without having to concentrate all the time.

Abnormalities are immediately visible, and the member of staff feels the need to pull the Andon, so the problems can be captured and eliminated.

The visibly underloaded process is normally allocated to a highly skilled staff member. A skilled staff member will be able to pause during the unallocated work time and study their and other processes and staff members' situations for potential problems or kaizen.

The process is then a visible priority for the next kaizen activity, so the processes can soon be done with four people instead of five.

CHAPTER 26

OPERATION RATIO

or

How to measure our output performance other than safety, quality, efficiency and cost?

DEFINITION

Operation Ratio is a simple calculation which can be performed minute by minute, hourly, weekly or monthly.

It is the actual good-quality output quantity of the process divided by the planned output and multiplied by 100.

$$\mathbf{OPR} = \frac{\textbf{Actual good-quality output} \times \mathbf{100\%}}{\textbf{Planned output}}$$

Output can be number of products/cases or documents processed, depending upon the type of work being done.

It is a measure of the third of the 5 business result priorities of any organisation.

1. Safety
2. Quality
3. **Delivery on time or *Being on plan**
4. Efficiency
5. Cost

* In the case of a complex project or similar-type office work, the measure used is usually the schedule achievement element of the obeya. (Covered in another chapter.)

PURPOSE

The people at the workplace or office can understand their performance numerically using this simple tool.

This is usually visualised in the workplace, either manually or electronically, so that everyone can see the real-time situation.

For example, on a real-time basis, the calculation illustrates how many parts should have been made at this point in the working shift (based upon Takt time or target cycle time) versus the actual output.

Achievement is achievement. Over time, it shows the trend of our performance. The interesting measurement for the staff members is the gap between plan and actual. (If OPR is calculated at 92%, we are interested in the 8% of losses.)

We discuss the use of the Production Control Board in another chapter on visualisation. The basis for the PC Board calculation is OPR (Operation Ratio).

It is important that the losses accounted for on the PC Board each hour are equal to the total losses shown by the OPR percentage for the hour.

The causes of the losses will naturally be a mixture of issues. Equipment breakdown, process errors, pace of work, parts or information delays and so on.

By grasping the causes of the losses as they actually happen, the staff members on the process can understand the important details of exactly what happened at the time of each loss. They will be able to resolve many issues for themselves but, where they cannot, this information is invaluable for their supporting engineers/specialists, and problem investigation time is dramatically reduced.

PLANNED VS UNPLANNED LOSSES

Well managed organisations will have specific time periods designated for such items as training, trials, equipment maintenance, etc. Where these times are within the scheduled working day, they are normally excluded from the OPR calculation. Thus, the staff members on the process can see their own process's performance reflected clearly.

These planned activities are as important as the process

output. They are the basis upon which good performance rests.

Reducing training or maintenance, for example, is a very short-term and dangerous method of increasing the time available for processing. When volume demand outstrips current performance capacity, this is too often the first port of call for management.

However, improving the methods of doing these tasks, and therefore reducing the time they take to be done properly, is an often neglected kaizen area.

One organisation which supplied parts to the automotive sector was quite advanced in the basic understanding of OPR and had excellent visualisation of the line's real-time performance.

One Monday morning, I was walking to the line we were working on with the Operations General Manager and noticed many lines were not operating. When I asked him what the issue was, he replied, "There is no issue, this is TPM time."*

Quite rightly, there was pride in his voice. This is a very advanced example of staff member development whilst doing the job. The production members were maintaining their equipment.

We were returning to the office as lunchtime approached. The lines were still not operating and I could see no one working on any of the equipment. I queried this, and he replied, "TPM time is from start of shift until lunchtime on each line."

Further discussion revealed that every line had the standard TPM time from start of shift to lunchtime and the team leader did most of the actual activity.

The excellent intention of TPM was to be applauded, but there were four clear and important opportunities:

1. *The TPM for each line could not possibly be exactly the same time.*

The evidence of no one on the lines prior to lunch showed that many lines were already finished. Production time was being wasted.

TPM is effective when well standardised and, therefore, the time required is very clear for each line. No time should be wasted.

2. *The team members were not completely involved in the TPM.*

   A very important opportunity for them to learn and develop was being missed.

   This is an imbalance between the two wheels of business progress and development of the people.

3. *The team member's time was seen to be unimportant to the company. It was OK for them not be fully engaged for a full half shift.*

   Their ownership and a sense of value were being lost without the conscious realisation of the management team.

4. *When all team members are engaged in the TPM activity the time required for completion is dramatically reduced.*

**TPM = Total Productive Maintenance, an advanced method in which production people get to know their equipment by doing the basic maintenance tasks themselves. This is a topic of its own.*

CHAPTER 27

PROJECT AND ANNUAL PLAN VISUAL MANAGEMENT

or

The obeya

THE OBEYA

The obeya is used to manage any activity which has clear time-bound objectives and which several different disciplines need to work together to achieve a good result.

It is ideal for managing projects of all types and also for managing the achievement of annual plans.

The tool is very powerful in achieving results on time, but also makes the achievement of continual performance improvement and staff member development in line with business priorities very clear.

Like the Direction Deployment tool explained in Chapter 8, these results becomes better and better with each cycle of use.

Also like other tools, it is the combination of many simpler tools, used in the correct context and sequence, which delivers the big added value.

The diagram which follows is a picture of a project obeya, showing all of the elements as they fit together.

The physical visualisation of an obeya follows this form to ensure all elements are present and used. In other words, this is an image of what an obeya looks like on a wall with each box being a document.

Project Obeya Image

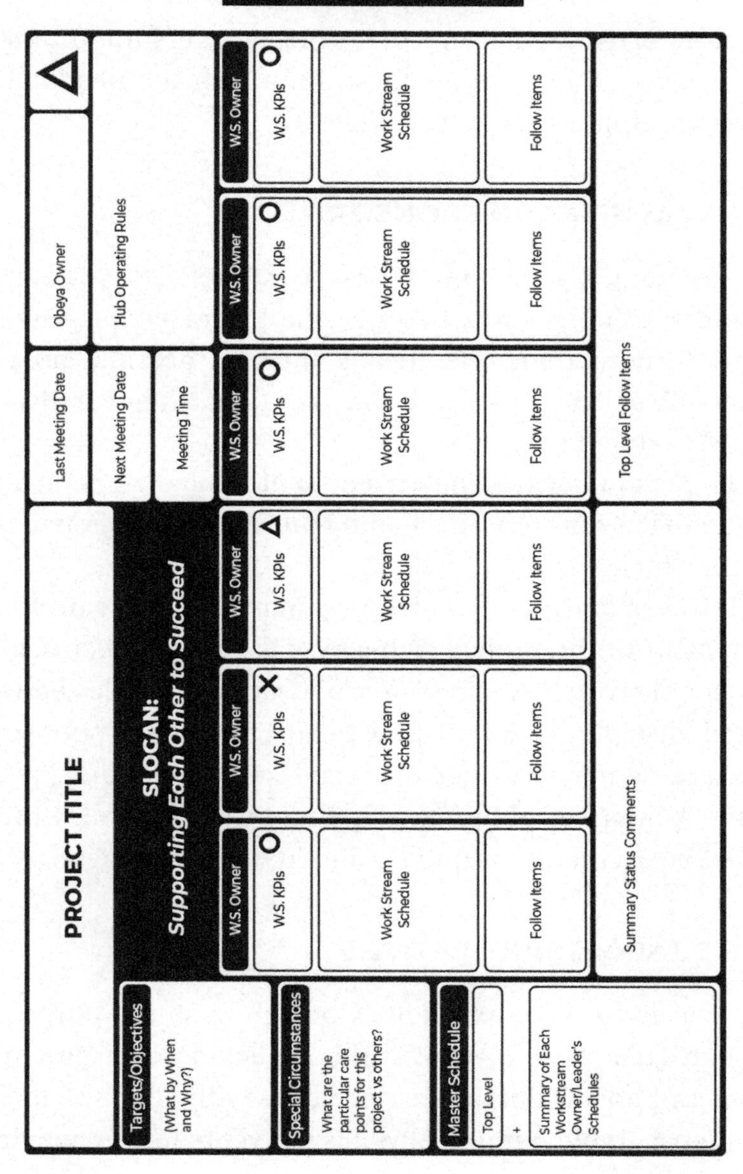

STEPS OF THE OBEYA

The order of using each step of the obeya is very important.

Creation of the obeya is best done with the heads of the related disciplines at the first stages.

STEP 1 OWNER AND SPONSOR

Who will actually lead and be responsible for the delivery of the project? There must be only one leader/owner. Division between more than one means there is actually no clear ownership or leadership. It cannot be a department or division. Always a named person.

The person does not need to be senior management, and it is better if it is not so, as the leading the obeya will often require full-time focus.

However, one member of the top management team should be sponsor of the project. Whenever the owner is struggling, for example with mixed resource allocation priorities between related disciplines, he or she needs to have a sponsor at sufficient seniority to get the issue sorted out quickly and finally. A member of top management who can talk with the related board members quickly and informally is ideal.

STEP 2 TARGETS/OBJECTIVES

This step is to reach consensus on the business purpose of this particular obeya. What is the expected achievement, by when, and how will it be measured? As with all of the tools, if it not measurable numerically, it is not yet ready for activity or delegation.

The meeting can take 30 minutes for a very experienced

team, to 4 hours for beginners.

The clarity and accuracy of this step will impact the outcome directly.

Very often, this document is revisited several times as the obeya preparation progresses. This is not a problem. It just means that the understanding of the situation and direction are being developed more and more. This alone is big added value.

The understanding of the disciplines needed to be included in the obeya can also be developed during this activity.

Here are two examples of targets and objective setting.

The first one is a very straightforward set of targets for a company which made manufacturing cells for other organisations. Each cell was unique and each one was a project in itself. You could say their core business was projects.

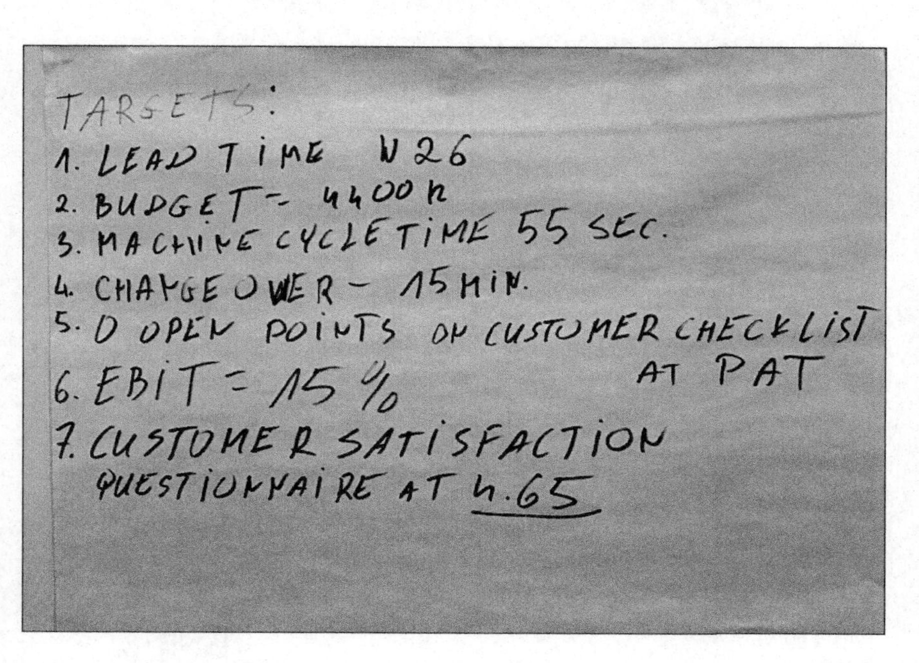

Example 1

The second is a much larger organisation which was using an obeya to coordinate a long-term activity of anticipating and meeting the changes in requirements of the customers and maximising the benefits of developments in technology over the coming decade.

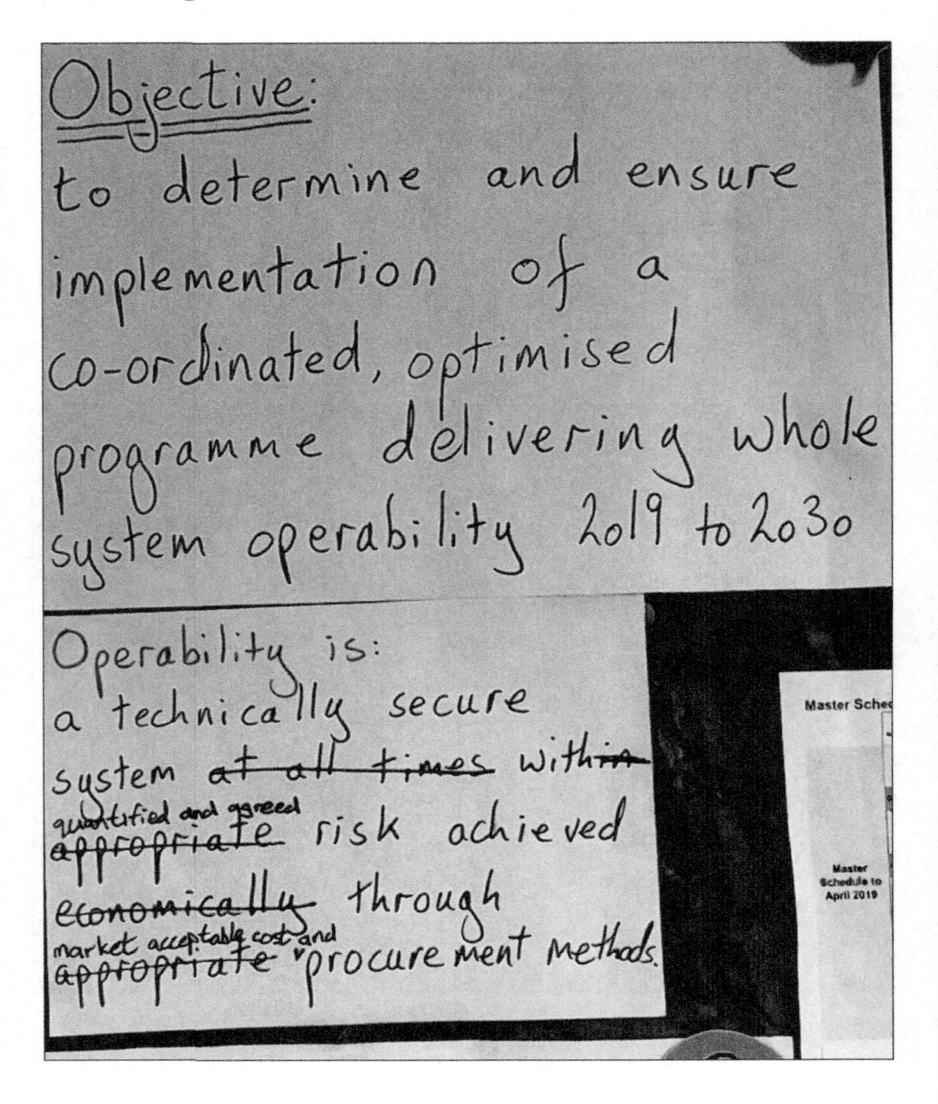

Example 2

Both examples, as you can see, were developed in rough before transferring to the obeya. This by far the best way for every step. Everything must be easy to challenge and develop.

The second example shows the team struggling to make the general term 'operability' measurable and quantifiable. They finally achieved it, but not on this example.

They then went on to tackle what they meant by 'coordinated' and 'optimised'. Until they had done so, it was unfair to begin delegating the activity to subordinates.

In both examples, during stage one it became very clear to everyone that the objective of the obeya was not the same in everyone's mind when they started the step.

At this stage the top level KPIs, by which success will be measured, are decided.

STEP 3 SPECIAL CIRCUMSTANCES

What are the things that need to be taken into account in achieving the outcome?

Some potential examples are:

- Are there legislative parameters which have to be met?
- Is something liable to change in the circumstance surrounding the project?
- What is unique about this project versus similar projects?

Special Circumstances

1. Cycle time
2. Specific shuttle system
3. 3D vision system
4. 2D fanuc system
5. ICV loading system
6. Cradle change over
7. New smart conveyor system
8. Tool change over
9. Cradle fixation on the lift
10. Specific welding unite for HSB component
11. Specific pick and place
12. Guarding type to be decided
13. QC connectors
14. Too many project in the same time
15. Suppliers management delivery on time

Example 1

In example 1, the unique items were mainly technical specification differences from previous projects. Each of these required action from design to clarify before other disciplines could make progress. Each item was added to the master schedule so that these decisions were taken in a timely manner.

Special Circumstances:

A small and business-flexible delivery date project milestone.

The product team has taken the challenge to make a **model of excellence in project management** which targets and delivers:

- **Quality of planning** with a view to **certainty of product quality.**
- **Efficient use of resources** by maintaining **sensibly planned timings.**
- **Delivery on or before** the **planned target date.**

  By:
- **Open, sincere and visual communication.**

Example 2

In example 2, the team decided that, as this was the first obeya their organisation had used, one of their special circumstances was to not only to achieve the objectives, but also to make a model for future dissemination.

STEP 4 DECIDE WORK STREAMS AND OWNERS

During the first 3 steps, the scope of the project, and therefore the nature and number of work streams needed to complete the work, will become clear.

In some projects, the work streams may simply be each related department or discipline. This is true, for example, when a new vehicle or product is being introduced to a manufacturing plant.

In other projects, there may be a need for a work stream which is made up of representatives of several disciplines working closely together. For example, when a decision is needed about which of the possible future scenarios is the one to be adopted for development activity.

In both cases, there, again, must be one named owner for each work stream. They, like the obeya owner, will be given whatever support they need to meet the obeya requirements.

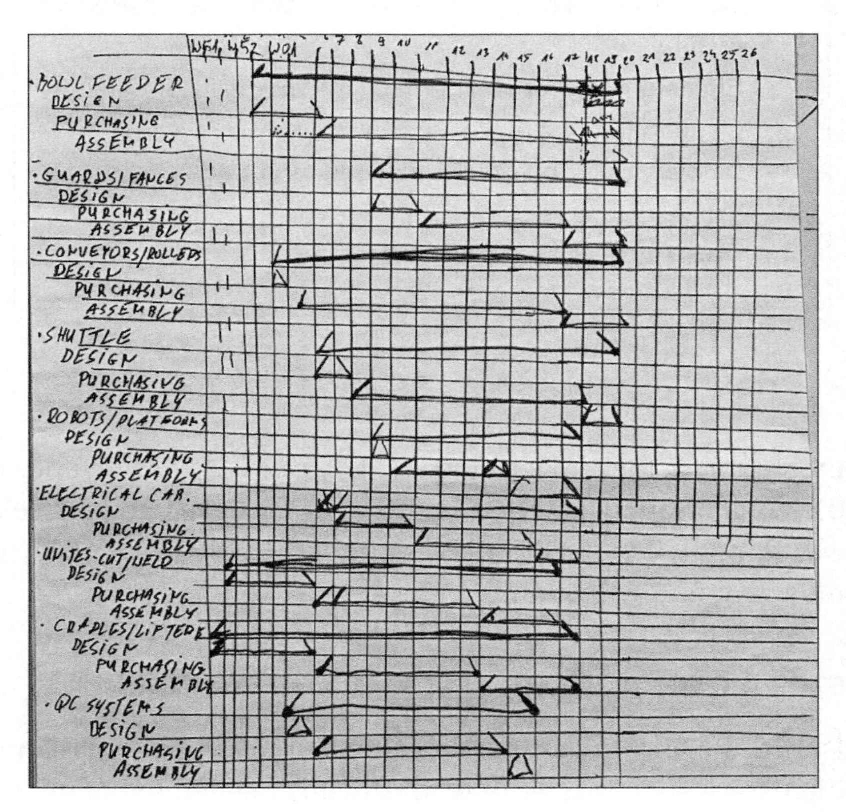

STEP 5 MAKE THE MASTER SCHEDULE

This step is the most important for success.

The key point is that the leaders of every work stream are actively involved in the making of the schedule.

The schedule making starts with agreeing the completion or delivery date of the obeya targets. This becomes a fixed point which can only be changed by the obeya owner in consultation with the sponsor. This is true whether the delivery date is a non-negotiable business need, or the consensus of the project leaders.

From the end date, the project leader and team work backwards making the major milestones which need to be achieved along the way.

The lead time needed for the delivery of each milestone is agreed between all related work streams. The lead times are used in working backwards through the milestones to the project start point. In projects without precedent experience, this often requires the work stream leaders to quickly decide their work stream members and to hold discussions with them first.

It is also not unusual for the first teams to use the obeya tool to discover that the start date has already passed. In this case, additional resource must be urgently provided to catch back up to the schedule.

Adherence to the completion date is the fixed point. From this, problems will become visible and problems resolved in time to meet it.

During the project, the meeting of each major milestone is treated in the same way as the completion date.

This is essential to manage resources between several projects effectively. Once milestones are allowed to slip, the organisation goes into 'doing what we can' mode, compromising plan after plan and having to redo each plan again and again or risk losing management control altogether.

In example 1, which follows, the work streams decided to make the completion of each sub-assembly element a major milestone.

The final steps prior to delivery were assembly of the whole line and then testing.

The assembly sequence and assembly process lead times provided the major milestone completion deadlines.

From these, each sub-assembly was traced back through their steps from delivery to the final assembly line through manufacturing, purchasing and design.

The lead times for each activity, e.g. manufacture, purchasing and design, provided the deadlines for one department to finish their work in order for the following departments to have sufficient time to do their work correctly. In project speak, the major dependencies become clearly defined.

The lead times decided must be enough for a correct and good-quality result. These lead times should not be challenged at this time. To do so simply removes ownership right from the start.

There are several small circled numbers at the top of the master schedule. These are the points at which the items marked as Special Circumstances need to be decided.

Yes, for this project, the necessary start point for activity was indeed earlier than the obeya preparation began. From the beginning, the project team recognised they needed to immediately begin catching back up.

Example 1

STEP 6 WORK STREAMS MAKE THEIR INDIVIDUAL SCHEDULES

Based upon the master schedule milestones, each work stream makes their own detailed schedule. At this time resource allocation can be done effectively, allowing multiple projects to be managed within each discipline.

Sometimes, after going into the details, this will expose that adjustments to the master schedule may be necessary.

The obeya owner is responsible for coordinating and authorising such changes. (The completion date cannot be changed without the authorisation of the project sponsor.)

The work stream's schedules must be shown in time elements short enough to be able to accurately judge the status for each meeting. Weekly elements are usually enough.

At this stage, the work streams can usually make their individual KPIs which will add up to the total obeya KPIs.

From the plans, the progress of KPI achievement during the obeya life can also be calculated and graphed for display.

STEP 7 THE OBEYA IS FORMALLY CONSTRUCTED

The formal obeya is physically made, usually on boards or walls, in the format shown in the first Obeya Image diagram. The overall format and the placing of the project-wide documents are the responsibility of the project owner. Each work stream owner is responsible for their own display.

The documents should be large enough for the schedules to be legible at 3 metres. This will be large enough for all attendees to grasp the content during the obeya stand-up meetings.

Experienced teams working on a project which is not a completely new in content will achieve this stage within 1.5 to 2 days from the first meeting of the discipline heads.

I have seen, even very new, teams achieve all the steps up to this point in 4 hours for subsequent obeyas, because much of the work can be carried over.

STEP 8 DECIDE THE OBEYA OPERATING PRINCIPLES

The team should discuss and reach consensus about what are the principles or rules with which the obeya meetings will be operated. The first 7 steps will add big value to any project, because they provide a structured framework for teamwork and ownership to be achieved. However, the resulting documents will not provide a good result by themselves, there is nothing magic about them.

The way in which the obeya is operated and managed also makes for success or failure.

Example 1 shows the operating rules which organisations find most effective.

Example *(opposite)*

Please note the importance of the Andon when using the obeya tool. Without it, the tool can easily become a source of intense and unhealthy pressure for the participants. (This is true of all effectively accountable management systems.)

STEP 9 PREPARATION FOR OBEYA WORKING MEETINGS

One day before each meeting, each work stream's schedule status is updated by the work stream owner. The work stream will also complete the follow-up item box for their responsibility.

The obeya owner can then update the master schedule based upon the work stream statuses and any related discussions/ clarifications.

The method of showing the schedule achievement status is a simple line down the schedule as shown in the next diagram.

OBEYA OPERATING RULES

- Meet frequently enough to keep control of achieving the Master Schedule. (Weekly, daily, etc. as the situation needs.)
- If an owner cannot attend, they must send a replacement who is able to report and to make decisions on their behalf at the meeting.
- Changes to a work stream schedule must be authorised by the work stream owner.
- Changes to the Master Schedule must be authorised by the obeya owner.
- Schedule changes where there is a dependency must be authorised by both related work stream owners.
- We all succeed, or we all fail. We are a team.
- We do whatever it takes to keep to the Master Schedule milestones.
- We use the Andon for:

    1. Potential delays to the Master Schedule.
    2. Potential workload difficulties.
    3. When help is needed.

- Start meetings on time.
- One voice at a time.
- We are all doing our best. Let us respect and support each other to succeed, always.

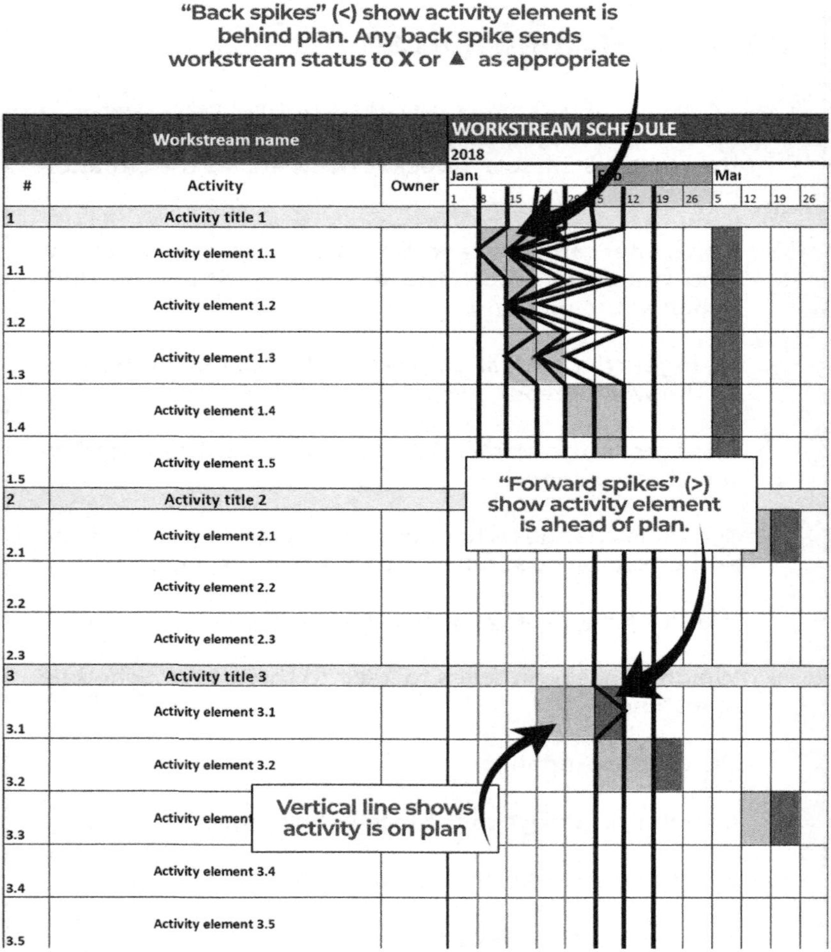

"Back spikes" (<) show activity element is behind plan. Any back spike sends workstream status to X or ▲ as appropriate

Workstream name			WORKSTREAM SCHEDULE												
			2018												
#	Activity	Owner	Jan					Feb				Mar			
			1	8	15	22	29	5	12	19	26	5	12	19	26
1	Activity title 1														
1.1	Activity element 1.1														
1.2	Activity element 1.2														
1.3	Activity element 1.3														
1.4	Activity element 1.4														
1.5	Activity element 1.5														
2	Activity title 2														
2.1	Activity element 2.1														
2.2	Activity element 2.2														
2.3	Activity element 2.3														
3	Activity title 3														
3.1	Activity element 3.1														
3.2	Activity element 3.2														
3.3	Activity element 3.3														
3.4	Activity element 3.4														
3.5	Activity element 3.5														

"Forward spikes" (>) show activity element is ahead of plan.

Vertical line shows activity is on plan

Each work stream and the total obeya will display their summary status using the circle/triangle/cross method described in the visualisation chapter.

The owner will then complete the obeya boxes for status summary comments and top level follow-up items.

These status indicators and comments will form the discussion items for the meeting. It is imperative that all issues are made visible.

In the early days, it may be helpful if the obeya and work stream owners confirm attendance of all the people they need to join the meeting. This will help people to form new, or to change old, habits. The obeya sponsor must attend the first 4 meetings to get the process off the ground and at least once per month after that. He or she should also be sure to attend if the obeya owner requests it.

STEP 10 THE OBEYA MEETING

Each work stream leader will explain their status to the rest of the attendees. They will start with the status of any follow-up items and then cover the total status for their responsibility and any issues they are facing. Three or four minutes is usually enough.

This is the point at which work stream owners should 'pull the Andon' where needed. This is the latest point for doing so. Issues should be raised with the obeya owner at the moment they become visible and appropriate support provided or action taken as necessary at the time.

This includes summoning the obeya sponsor if needed.

The obeya owner will ensure that all necessary further follow-up items are recorded during the meeting, with clear ownership and due dates.

After all work streams have reported, the obeya owner will explain the top level follow-up items completion and total obeya status, including the Master Schedule. Any further top level follow-up items will be confirmed and the summary status points explained.

The sponsor may decide to make some appreciation, direction or clarification prior to the obeya owner closing the meeting.

CONTINUOUS IMPROVEMENT

The obeya system should provide positive progress in not only on-time delivery and KPI achievement, but should also lead to improvements in the management of 'project'-type activities.

The first model change project Toyota UK managed required 18 months to implement. Even then, recovering performance KPI to pre-change levels required a further 3 months after the start of production.

As the project was implemented the obeya owner, each work stream owner and each team made simple check sheets showing the steps needed to complete delivery on time and at good quality. For each step, the key points and length of time needed was also noted.

At each major milestone, all participants made a formal PDCA review of the previous steps and the check sheets were modified to incorporate any improvement items identified.

These check sheets became the Process Memory or standardised work sheets for the next project.

The availability of these check sheets (you may have heard of them referred to as Keshi-Komi) often enabled more junior members of the organisation to take responsible roles in a project as they could follow the standard.

Using this method, the time required for new model introduction improved, step by step, until a new model could be brought to production in 6 months. Recovery of performance took a week.

The frequency of new model projects was much lower for each of the 3 European engine/transmission plants. A gap of 10 years was not uncommon between major changes. After completing the PDCA cycle, each plant formally handed over the revised Keshi-Komi from their last project to the plant with the next one.

In this way, the performance of every plant improved at 3 times the pace than would have otherwise been the case.

SECTION THREE
MOVING TO PROGRESSIVE

Moving from Kaizen to Visionary

CHAPTERS 28 TO 34 COVER THE STEPS FROM PROACTIVE TO PROGRESSIVE MATURITY

CHAPTER 28

PROACTIVE TO PROGRESSIVE

or

Flexibility and the ability to focus on the long term

Moving through Stabilising and Proactive maturity will have changed the very nature of any organisation.

Particularly we, the top management members, will be viewing everything with a different set of eyes than previously. The priorities we have for our time will have moved from the traditional reporting meeting and office-based schedules to a Go and See, coaching and developing style. The use of obeyas and other visual management tools, plus shorter and more efficient meetings, will have freed up diary time to do this.

Our own eyes will quickly see waste in all its forms and our ability to permanently solve problems will have been honed to the point where it is natural.

By now, our people will be capable of much more than we previously imagined. We will have liberated resource, previously tied up in daily activities, to enable us to form an increasingly knowledgeable central team of internal masters to accelerate the pace of development and performance improvement.

Proactive to Progressive

PROACTIVE		PROGRESSIVE
Stakeholders see good management		**Stakeholders follow management**

PROACTIVE

Stakeholders see good management

- Targets regularly achieved
- One team
- Big problem solving capacity at the shop floor
- Seven wastes reducing
- Fewer and fewer problems
- Planned maintenance done religiously
- People more and more professional
- Changes anticipated and managed
- Customer is king
- Good analysis of facts drives direction
- Future vision and plans clear to all

Performance breaking new boundaries

PROGRESSIVE

Stakeholders follow management

- Challenge targets regularly achieved
- Everyone involved achieving Vision
- TPM in place and maintenance costs reducing safely
- People are professionals
- Processes learn from experience
- Problem-solving skills used also to make concrete plans
- Performance step change done regularly
- Capacity increasing at no extra cost
- New business opportunities can be sought and managed quickly

Flexibility and additional capacity

Particularly, the knowledge and practical application of TPS tools at an organisation-wide and at the very local level will have progressed, as always, in line with the business priorities.

Our respect for, and therefore our expectations of, our people will be continually growing, so that the level of challenge the organisation can manage will grow also.

By this time, the smoothness and reliability of the standard daily activities will have already removed much of the stress from the workforce and management. An atmosphere of calm progress will prevail.

There will be a firm and practical application of policies and procedures, even if some particular circumstances make this more expensive or difficult to do.

'Expediency' will be replaced by all levels knowing that they can make decisions based upon policy and procedures with confidence and security.

At this point, we can rely on our organisation to deliver the annual direction dissemination and projects on time and the performance results we are looking for.

This will remain true as long as we personally and methodically maintain the new habits of structured and regular visualisation, Go and See, responding immediately to an Andon and coaching. These responsibilities can never be delegated successfully.

The top management support team or corporate office will have standardised the working calendar and management methods, so we can have time to think more systemically and with a farther horizon.

Our scope of opportunity can now move to:

FLEXIBILITY

- Rapid response to changes.
- Minimum investment and losses during times of change.

BUILT-IN PERFORMANCE

- Zero safety and quality problems and zero unplanned equipment losses.

INCREASING COMPETITIVENESS

- Benchmarking.
- Breakthrough challenges.

LONG AND WIDE PERSPECTIVE

- Minimum 10-year strategy making.
- Creating the mission.

CHAPTER 29

FLEXIBILITY

or

Maximum speed & minimum losses during change

MANPOWER FLEXIBILITY

If the workload changes, so should the number of man-hours spent doing the required work.

In reality, we know that larger organisations do not find headcount numbers to be so flexible. For example, even during large reductions in the workload required to meet customers' requirements, it is seldom cost-efficient to release employees and rehire them in any period less than 6 months. Where redundancy payments are involved, this can change to more than a year.

This is based upon the simplistic calculation of cost to release and cost to rehire. When the loss of accumulated skill and development are included, the benefits of even medium-term headcount reductions come into question.

From another basic viewpoint, every moment of an individual's life is too precious to be wasted.

Man-hours available, but not required for the immediate workload, should be spent doing other value-added activities, especially in improving safety, quality, efficiency and, through them, costs. Remember that temporary manpower reduction saves money only once. Kaizen savings repeat for every piece of work done from that point onwards, year after year.

Surplus man-hours, which remain in the workplace when workload reduces, and which are not accumulated and reassigned to other value-added tasks, actually make front line management's job much harder. I know that this is completely counter-intuitive, even for front line management, but it is so. The surplus hours generate their own difficulties in maintaining the disciplines TPS depends upon. (Please see the section on process rebalancing in Chapter 25 – The Full Man Process).

Process rebalancing is an essential element of kaizen.

Through this, unnecessary man-hours can be seen and quickly reallocated from the original workplace to other value-added work. Rebalancing can take place between teams as well as within them. In this way, unnecessary time can be accumulated to reallocate the maximum number of people.

Keeping 'positive tension' in the teams and groups by process rebalancing is very important. It also introduces the need for each staff member to be able to perform as many process elements as possible within the team and even across teams.

MULTI-SKILLING

Maintaining good safety, quality and efficiency whilst responding quickly to changes in demand, manpower availability and work content are an important part of true flexibility. They are also a source of pride and motivation for employees.

It is important enough to make it a practical and standardised part of management at all levels and disciplines.

TOYOTA EXAMPLE

The simple method of visualising and managing this issue, used by Toyota, has yet to be bettered in my experience, so I offer it here as one example.

It is called a Versatility Chart and is used universally throughout the corporation.

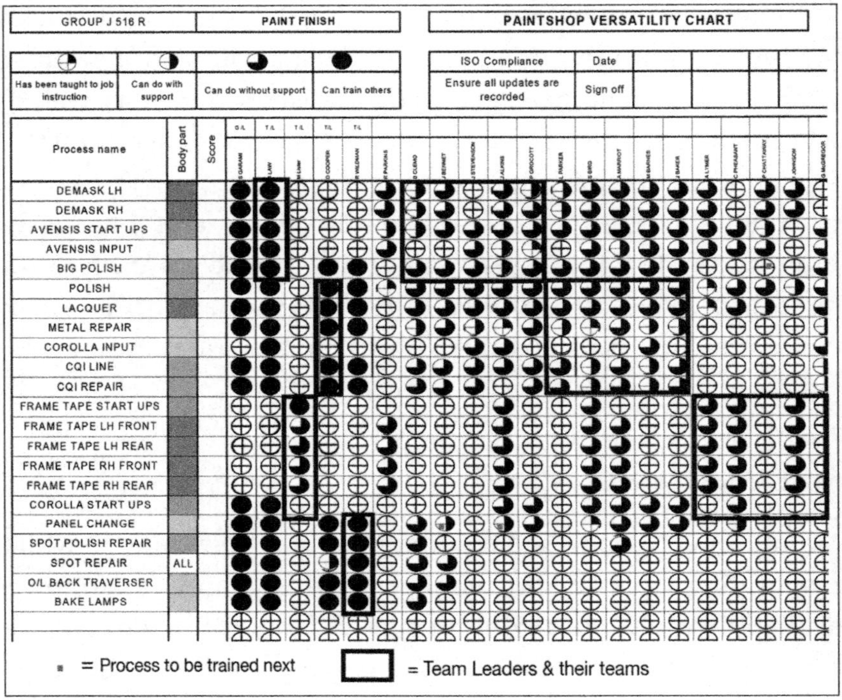

GROUP J 516 R | PAINT FINISH | PAINTSHOP VERSATILITY CHART

Has been taught to job instruction | Can do with support | Can do without support | Can train others

ISO Compliance | Date
Ensure all updates are recorded | Sign off

Process name | Body part | Score

O/L | T/L | T/L | T/L | T/L

DEMASK LH
DEMASK RH
AVENSIS START UPS
AVENSIS INPUT
BIG POLISH
POLISH
LACQUER
METAL REPAIR
COROLLA INPUT
CQI LINE
CQI REPAIR
FRAME TAPE START UPS
FRAME TAPE LH FRONT
FRAME TAPE LH REAR
FRAME TAPE RH FRONT
FRAME TAPE RH REAR
COROLLA START UPS
PANEL CHANGE
SPOT POLISH REPAIR
SPOT REPAIR ALL
O/L BACK TRAVERSER
BAKE LAMPS

= Process to be trained next
= Team Leaders & their teams

Versatility Chart

FOR A LARGER VERSION AND MORE RESOURCES, VISIT
WWW.CARLKLEMM.COM

This visualisation is used for office and shop floor roles. This truncated example is from the paint shop repair area, red shift. The charts cover one group or office section. Each team leader is responsible for updating their people's status and plan on a monthly basis. It looks complex but in fact is very simple.

The left-hand column is skills. The group leader and then team leaders are the first of the subsequent columns then each team member.

The skill level judgement is universal and pretty functional. Does the team member have the skill to work alone or not? Can

they train others? In this case, you can see that only the team leaders can train. As the group matures, more team members will be taught the Toyota Job Instruction method so that they can also train their well-established skills to others.

Simply by looking at staff members with three segments on any skill, the G/L can confidently arrange the day's manning for each process with their team leaders and arrange support for the day's training.

Once a month, the group and team leaders gather to confirm the previous month's plan achievement and to confirm the next month's training plans. In the office this meeting would be the manager and their assistant managers or section managers.

The paint shop assistant manager and above can quickly see the skill condition of the group as they pass the group's status board. No further documentation or reporting is required. No need to disturb the group leader and his people from their important work.

Incidentally, as you can see, the team leaders are required to be able to perform all of their team's roles and to be able to train them. They also personally cover planned and unplanned absence in their team. In this way, they retain their practical knowledge and skills and can keep up to date with all kaizen. Also, they can quickly identify and support any team members that may be struggling or operating incorrectly.

Breaking each role into its component elements for training and multi-skilling enables quick manpower adjustment. Changes in order levels can be met by moving the elements as required, to increase or decrease the manning as needed.

Losses, which might otherwise have been caused by having to learn new skills after a change, are avoided by members of the workforce being able to do many elements within and outside their own role.

Which elements can be moved are usually concentrated on 'pebble' elements. That is to say, elements which will not result in any role being unable to complete a task from start to finish. Individual ownership of a good result should never be compromised.

Departments at the Progressive level have usually experienced many changes in workload and can identify five or six 'preferred' configurations of process rebalance which result in the maximum effective use of manpower. These can then be planned and prepared for as part of the normal skills matrix process. Changes which fall in between these configurations are met by adopting the closest 'preferred' option.

Of course, these will change over time as more and more kaizen are implemented.

In addition to guaranteeing consistency of performance, standardisation of roles, in all types of work, goes a long way to liberate organisations from dependency upon individual employee's skills.

It also means that many elements of tasks can be allocated to staff members with less skill and experience, allowing them to make an increased contribution to their organisation. The value-added contribution of the highest skilled and experienced staff members can then be increased by allowing them to spend more of their time on the work which requires their special abilities.

FACILITY FLEXIBILITY

Responding to changes in volume, mix or specification of work very often involves adjusting layout of equipment to facilitate different process sequencing, manning levels or job element combinations. The changeover time is a loss. Most organisations try to do this during non-working time, especially at weekends. This requires careful planning and management to reach the changeover point as intended.

Involving as many members of the working team as possible in the actual changeover reduces the time, if not the total man-hours, taken. In these cases, the changeover can often be completed in the time between working shifts.

Making equipment modular, self-contained, and, as much as possible, manually moveable at the concept and design stage is one of production engineering's important consideration points.

Power and other service supplies also designed to be easily moved is part of the facility design department's consideration points.

For organisations with facilities in many locations, such as the big, global corporations, there is another aspect to facility flexibility. Each location has its own set of circumstances: salary levels, skills availability, legislation, resources, maturity, market, etc. Each facility will benefit best from different levels of work complexity and also, incidentally, with different levels of automation.

MAINTENANCE FLEXIBILITY

Routine maintenance is frequently controlled by time period. For example, an electric motor is designated to be serviced every 6 months. This is an inflexible system. When workload changes, the equipment use can vary dramatically within any given time period.

Controlling routine maintenance by the number of equipment operation cycles automatically adjusts maintenance frequency and, hence, costs and also provides a practical basis for calculating required maintenance manpower.

Involving every production member in the routine inspection and maintenance of the equipment they use (TPM) not only enables their involvement in changeovers, but also dramatically increases their engagement, ownership and development.

The maintenance department members keep their leadership regarding the total TPM work allocation and also train the production people and certify their skill.

SUPPLY FLEXIBILITY

The steady and sustained elimination of losses caused by safety, quality and equipment problems during the Stabilising and Proactive stages of maturity will have resulted in very substantial reductions in the level of finished and in-process inventory needed to be held on site.

As the ability to stabilise internal performance increases, the organisation can begin to share the learning and develop the thinking and performance of its suppliers and service providers. Naturally, this will be done in the priority order of those suppliers which have the most impact on current total performance. The inventory held at suppliers can therefore also be reduced.

The inventory reduction will improve the lead time to change volumes and also to meet changes in the mix or design specifications of the workload. It will also reduce any losses caused when there is a need to adjust to sudden or unforeseen downturns in volume of work of any particular type.

A review of the planned inventory level should be carried out whenever significant performance improvements are made through problem-solving or kaizen activities.

Smallest possible delivery lot sizes, or Just In Time thinking is also important. Changing logistics methods, from supplier delivers to customer collects using 'milk runs' from several suppliers, largely eliminates the increased transportation costs that smaller lot sizes might otherwise appear to generate. The smaller lot sizes dramatically reduce the volume of inventory in the system.

For example, frequent deliveries, packaged in a way suitable for immediate transfer to the workplace, dramatically reduce the inventory level needed from receiving to use.

In Toyota plants this is usually half a shift, or four hours, maximum.

CHAPTER 30

BUILT-IN PERFORMANCE

or

Safety, quality and environment

ZERO SAFETY AND QUALITY PROBLEMS (BUILT-IN SAFETY)

Safety and quality are the two elements of any organisation where performance accurately measures the connection of management to the employees and the maturity of the development activities.

When an organisation reaches Progressive maturity, the achievement of zero accidents and zero defects plus, more recently, minimum environmental impact, all become possible whilst, at the same time, minimising costs.

All of these elements also rely almost entirely upon the priority which management gives to them, on a minute-by-minute and day-by-day basis, in every decision they make and in everything they say and do.

Clear and real Direction Deployment activities supported by strongly held policies, plus an ingrained balance between performance progress and staff member development, form the common foundations for the achievement and sustainment of all of these elements.

Each of the elements has unique tools and underlying assumptions which are important to understand.

SAFETY

An underlying assumption about safety is that no one consciously decides to hurt themselves.

(Of course, there may be mental or emotional issues which make this statement untrue for some individuals. These situations require a separate course of actions to resolve, often requiring specialist professional intervention.)

If the underlying assumption is true, then there are two

major causes of safety issues:

1. Lack of awareness of a danger.
2. Unconscious exposure to a known danger.

Addressing these two causes is the challenge.

1. LACK OF AWARENESS OF A DANGER

A driving instructor does not only teach and familiarise their students about how to operate a car, a very large part of their role is to educate them about the hazards of driving in public which are very different from any other hazards they may have previously known.

In every organisation, there are likewise many hazards, or dangers, with which their people are unfamiliar. Left to their own devices, each person will eventually learn what they are, but some of these lessons will be learned through a bad experience.

The challenge for the organisation is for the staff members to learn the dangers as quickly as possible, including how to avoid exposure to them.

There are many ways to do this. Let me share one practical method.

Each employee in Toyota takes part in frequent and regular, planned, KYT sessions.

Usually once per week.

(KYT is an acronym for the strangely mixed phrase 'Kiken Yochi Training.' Kiken = Danger or hazard. Yochi = Awareness.)

It is an activity for the local team in each workplace. It takes 10 to 15 minutes.

The team gather at a whiteboard and, initially, are shown a sketch or picture in which many obvious hazards are visible.

Each team member takes a turn identifying one of them. These are written on the whiteboard. The turn-by-turn identification continues until all of the team members have said "pass" because they can identify no more.

Then each team member, in turn, allocates one vote to the hazard they think is the biggest danger. The hazard with the most votes is then written as the focus point.

Each team member then takes a turn in proposing a method of removing or, as a minimum, avoiding the hazard during their work. The same method of saying "pass" is used to show when the list is finished. Then the team members vote upon which is the best and most practical proposal. If it is a way of removing the hazard, volunteers are sought to do that activity the same day. Otherwise, the session ends with all the team members forming a circle and touching left hands in the centre and pointing with their right hands whilst declaring "Yoshi!" (Let's do it!).

After a few initial sessions, the team will focus upon an area of their actual workplace or environs, instead of a pre-prepared image. By this time, their ability to identify hazards is much more developed, as is their sensitivity to smaller hazards.

It is a very simple and unthreatening, joint learning method.

Active mental engagement in not only identifying new hazards, but also how to remove or avoid them, promotes awareness and good habits. Using paid working time clearly says how important the subject is. Group leaders, assistant managers and managers each joining the activity of one of their teams, in rotation, makes the importance even clearer.

When the plant reached Progressive maturity, the KYT was replaced with similar meetings around the working area, but with the learning experiences of other teams, which had been published by the health and safety function, being shared at the first opportunity. The team then confirming their own area for such hazards and carrying out preventive actions. As company president, I would join the vice presidents, general manager, manager, etc., in meeting with each of their group leaders in rotation, to review their activities with them and to appreciate their staff member's efforts and results for safe working. I did this every day, and it would enable me to see every group around once per year.

This formal and prioritised use of the management team's time sent a very clear message to all members of staff regarding the importance of safe working:

"Put your body where your priorities are."

The plant's problem escalation standard meant that even minor incidents, which did not require any treatment, were notified to me immediately, and the top team would go to grasp first-hand what actually happened, so that when the countermeasure was reported the next day, we could easily judge the quality of the analysis and actions.

Not everyone has the same viewpoint. At one location, the national and local governments took a very different view of how to improve safety.

Everything had to be fully and formally risk assessed and all hazards documented by specialist safety engineers. A truly Napoleonic stance.

When an incident happened, the emphasis was on finding the person to be held responsible and taking commensurate corrective actions against them in terms of fines or loss of position. Was the documentation insufficient? If so, the management team were liable. Was the documentation correct but not followed? Then it was the fault of the person doing the task. I was once told by the local government head of safety, who incidentally was a very good and professional person in every respect, that he was concerned that I should be able to demonstrate that the company had taken formal corrective actions regarding safety, or the official judgement of my own performance as plant president could be at risk. He had taken the time and trouble to deeply understand our methods and agreed with them, but could not find a way to bring the two viewpoints into harmony.

2. UNCONSCIOUS EXPOSURE TO A KNOWN DANGER

Consciously or unconsciously, most staff members are very keen to be seen to perform well. Getting the job done as quickly and as easily as possible is an entirely natural approach.

Familiarity with the task being undertaken and a history of safe and successful completion leads to a more relaxed approach, compared with the first few times it is done.

It is under these circumstances that the safe, standardised steps can be unconsciously overlooked and incidents happen.

Where the performance of part, or all, of the organisation is at risk until the task is completed, such as a machine breakdown, pressure is added to the normal approach and multiplies by many times the chances of an incident.

This is the most difficult of safety issues to overcome, because it is seated deep in the subconscious.

It requires repeated reinforcement of the need to stop and consider before starting any task. The dangers of unconscious exposure can be well understood by the staff members, but understanding them will not be effective in emergency or high-pressure situations.

It is at these times when management must strongly insist upon a standard STOP and CONSIDER step in all actions. Even to the extent of being with the person when they are about to start the job and doing this step with them. This highly visible prioritisation and reinforcement is essential.

THE PROCESS MEMORY

The speed of learning and the consistency of safe working is too low in organisations which rely upon individual skill and experience.

Specific learning being captured by the process itself, so that everyone who does the process will do so in a proven, safe way, becomes an essential element of safety at work.

The Process Memory is described in Chapter 7.

The ownership of the Process Memory by the team responsible for that particular process is the thing which provides the effectiveness of the tool.

It is not unusual for management to delegate the preparation of the Process Memory, or Work Standards document, to a team of internal experts or engineers, especially to work study engineers. This can give management a sense of control and confidence and also of security regarding the discharge of their responsibilities for employee safety. However, it is a false sense, because the reality of work practice and the work standards documents very quickly become disconnected. Ten minutes at the workplace, comparing the two on any process, will make this clear.

Even with ownership in the correct place, there is still an important role for the management team to demonstrate the priority of this tool by physically confirming the transfer of learning to the Process Memory documents after a learning occasion, such as a safety incident, has happened. Even further, to then confirm that the team members performing the process have been trained in the new method, know why the change was made and are actually doing the process in the new way.

As top management, this confirmation is impossible for each learning occasion, but it is essential for us to perform a sampling process on important incidents, which assures us that the middle management and lower management are playing their part effectively.

These confirmations are easily dropped or overlooked without immediate consequences. Think of them as essential maintenance of the foundations of the organisation. They are that important.

ZERO DEFECTS (BUILT-IN QUALITY)

During the journey towards Progressive maturity level, as quality improves, the usual measures of defects per unit gradually become obsolete and are replaced by percentage defects.

With time, this measure also becomes obsolete and defects per million units becomes the appropriate measuring scale.

From this point, zero defects becomes a feasible concept.

At this point, the number of defects upon which to base the root cause and countermeasure investigation become less and less, and finally only one-off defects are available.

The problem-solving methods learned during the earlier stages no longer need the prioritisation step, and the investigation becomes immediate and much more forensic. High levels of logical analysis are required, based upon deep analysis of the defect and the surrounding circumstances.

These will still be done by the local team, but, more often, support may be required from specialist or expert resources.

The method of capturing the learning remains the Process Memory. Through clear and well followed standardisation most defects can be permanently eliminated.

There are some special concepts which, when used as tools, strongly support Built-In Quality. They are:

- Jidoka
- Jikotei Kanketsu

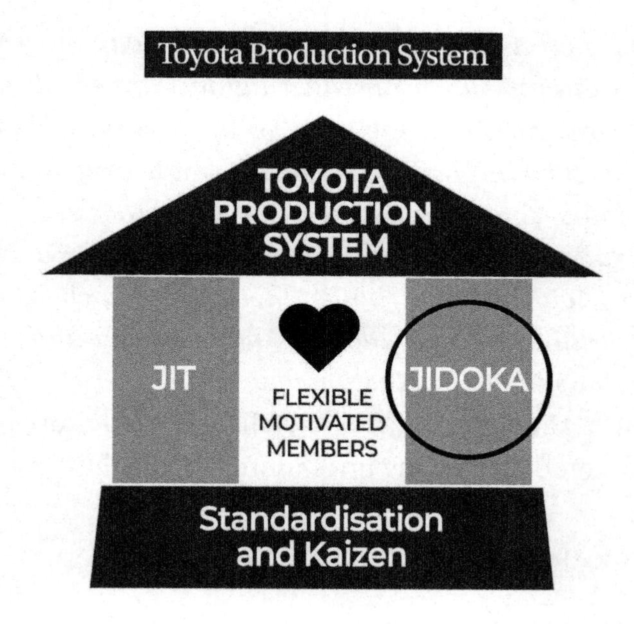

JIDOKA

The concept of Jidoka is one of the two pillars of the famous Toyota Productions System 'house'.

It originally represented the ability to separate man work from machine work by designing equipment which would automatically stop if a defect was detected. Thus, it was no longer necessary to employ one person per machine to watch over the process. One person could operate five or more machines without risking defects being made.

It was described as 'autonomation'.

The meaning has since broadened to the concept of **never**

passing a defect to the next process. This means stopping the process whenever there is a doubt about the quality of the output.

This tool, used to practise this concept, is explained in more detail in Chapter 10 'The Andon'.

Giving permission to stop the process was an anathema for organisations which operated tightly connected processes, such as conveyor lines. The number of stops each hour made continuous flow impossible. Problems would flow to the end of the line and be found, or not, by inspection processes.

By dividing the single, very long conveyor into 5 or 6 smaller conveyors, with a small buffer in between each of them, it became possible to apply the full Andon system and maintain manageably smooth production flow.

Modern AI methods have made Jidoka even more powerful and automated processing lines more flexible than ever before.

JIKOTEI KANKETSU

Jikotei Kanketsu is the twin sibling of Jidoka.

It is the concept of each process being in control of the quality of its output.

Dividing up the total production process into whole units of work, the quality of each unit should be able to be accurately judged by the person or equipment doing the process.

Judgement methods and criteria are essential elements of the process design.

In Chapter 25, we talk about rebalancing processes after kaizen in order to realise the benefits in terms of Full Man Process and efficiency. Originally, the major controlling factor for this was simply maintaining the necessary sequence of processes required to enable uninterrupted completion of the whole product. (For example, it makes no sense to assemble the seats into the vehicle before it has been painted.)

With Jikotei Kanketsu, the contents of each process are carefully combined so that the staff member doing the task has ownership of a whole 'unit' of the product.

For example, fitting the headlamp to a car. The headlamp has to be correctly located and fully secured, plus it has to be correctly connected to the electricity supply of the vehicle plus the connection has to be waterproof. This means that 4 clipping and 2 screwing elements have to be completed successfully and completely. It is not possible to see if the clips are fully engaged, so under the Jikotei Kanketsu concept, the designers make sure that the clips click loudly when correctly home. The screws can be seen to be fully home or not. The electrical connection likewise makes a clear clicking noise when fully located and the waterproofing boot can be seen to be in place correctly.

These elements are all part of the whole good-quality result for the headlamp fit and function. Therefore, under Jikotei Kanketsu, they would never be separated during process rebalancing activity. Instead, small and unrelated items we called 'pebble elements' could be moved freely within the appropriate work sequence.

Jikotei Kanketsu also operates at a much more macro level. The total vehicle quality is made up of many such smaller level Jikotei Kanketsu elements.

My first leader and sensei in Toyota returned to Japan, after his term in the UK, and became head of assembly for one of the largest plants. He was searching for a challenge for a plant which was already at full Proactive maturity.

Every plant at that time had a series of end of assembly tests, mainly functional items which could not be confirmed during the normal process.

One such test was the shower test. 'Shower' always made me smile, because it involved a 2000 litre per minute water deluge of the finished vehicle.

He challenged the plant to find a way that this test was no longer required.

"Can we make Jikotei Kanketsu for the waterproofing of our vehicles?"

A small coordinating team worked with the every department and function involved in this challenge. From the pressing shop, where body panels would have to align within 0.5 millimetres to ensure no welding problems, through the body shop fitting of doors and trunk lid and paint shop sealing of all of the joints, to the assembly shop where dozens of parts and seals had to be fitted perfectly. Naturally, this involved the design and production engineers, plus each of the suppliers which made related components.

Each element needed to understand, in concrete terms, what was needed in the process to assure no leaks on the finished vehicle. Each had to be self-reliant in the ability to judge a good condition.

It took almost a year, but finally it was very proudly achieved.

During the whole activity, each of the processes and people involved strongly developed their understanding of Jikotei Kanketsu and also their own abilities and skills. The processes were improved without costs increasing. The cost of the shower test was eliminated. The balance of excellence between business benefit and people development, at the Progressive level of maturity, was achieved.

(Incidentally, the sensei went on to become an executive vice president of Toyota Corporation.)

This concept of Jikotei Kanketsu is also very much in play when designing office-type processes, especially in the areas of decision-making, ensuring that the full process is followed based upon all relevant facts, logical thinking and thorough consultation.

CHAPTER 31

INCREASING COMPETITIVENESS

INCREASING COMPETITIVENESS

Until now, we have talked about the things which an organisation can do to improve its performance and the development of its people from a mainly inward-looking perspective. Each step, Stabilising and Proactive, may have included challenges to the norms of some organisations.

The Progressive organisation is now in a position to look outside and find new opportunities. Also to challenge previously unimaginable objectives which exceed all accepted limitations.

LOOKING OUTWARD

Ensuring the continual improvement of the performance and effectiveness of our organisations is only one of our many top management roles, as I am sure you already know.

The discussion, so far, has been almost exclusively about activities which are internally focused.

For organisations which have reached Proactive maturity, the next big opportunities come from having time and strong resources to grasp what is happening outside, in the rest of the world.

No matter how good our own progress is, there are always other organisations which are doing some, or all, of the things *we* are proud of, or not so proud of, better than us. Here is a source of many new challenges and opportunities which, for the most part, we may have been unable to imagine for ourselves.

BENCHMARKING

Any visit to another facility can be a benchmarking visit, if we choose to make it so. It is a mindset that can be cultivated by the top management team and which will be absorbed into the organisation's culture.

A precursor to any visit to another organisation, for whatever reason, was the 60-second briefing from the senior person attending to the other attendees. "Remember, it is very easy and feels very nice to identify all the things that our organisation does better than the one we are visiting. This is non-value added. Please be prepared to explain, during our journey home, a minimum of five things that this organisation does better than we do. They do not have to be big things." As a result of this, our people looked with a different set of eyes and invariably learned many new tools and approaches that helped us to move forward faster than would otherwise have been the case.

Benchmarking is most valuable during the strategy making period, but is also useful when a function or division is struggling to meet objectives.

Identifying the right organisation to benchmark may take a little research and agreeing benchmarking visits often entails offering a reciprocal visit. It is a balance, but one which is usually well worth the effort.

For larger organisations, benchmarking between facilities is much easier and always worthwhile.

For organisations seeking to understand the practical meaning of bringing the set of management tools together, the opportunity to benchmark an organisation which has already done so is extremely helpful.

For this reason, when I was head of Toyota's engine unit plant in Deeside, North Wales, I wanted to provide such a facility. Transferring what I had learned, in Toyota, to other organisations, in order to increase their competitiveness, was part of my motivation for joining the corporation from the very beginning.

The timing was right for such an open benchmarking opportunity in Deeside, as it was immediately after the 2008 global market disaster and we had many highly skilled members of staff available. Doing so required permission from Toyota's executive vice president for global manufacturing.

We benchmarked a similar facility in North America, prepared the A3 proposal for a 'Toyota Lean Management Centre' and I went to talk with him. He said, "No, please focus on your core business." After several further visits and discussions, during which we had the opportunity to explain how such a facility would not only be very much welcomed in Europe, but would also provide an excellent development opportunity for our own people - nothing develops conscious and structured learning better than helping other organisations to implement what you already do - he agreed, based upon the balance of sharing externally and developing our people by the same activity.

I moved away from the Deeside facility in 2010, but the centre has continued to grow and develop and now offers many targeted training and hands-on experiences, plus support for transferring the tools and principles back to the client organisation. The centre has worked with more than 450 organisations and done extensive work with Enterprise Ireland and also the Welsh Development Agency in supporting their domestic organisations.

The unique point for all of the offerings is that they are conducted in a full Toyota facility and Go and See the actual condition is an integral part of every curriculum.

Googling TLMC will bring up the home page for Toyota Lean Management Centre.

CHALLENGING ACCEPTED LIMITATIONS

At the Progressive stage of maturity, the words "That is impossible" and "We will never be able to do that" are music to the ears! They make the pulse rate rise and the eyes shine.

When a new engine, to replace the current one, was to be introduced because of tightening European emissions regulations, the corporation told me that the revisions would mean a minimum 150 euro increase in the price of the unit. Every plant and sales organisation was struggling with profitability in a time of low volumes and high competition. This was a substantial cost increase to pass on to the customer!

After discussion, our management team reached consensus to challenge introducing the new unit at zero cost increase.

"Impossible!"

It wasn't just about improving competitiveness, it was the type of challenge the members of the plant had grown to relish.

Every department and division in the company joined in the quest. Everyone in the organisation studied their work, step-by-step, over many months. Our staff members not only challenged their own work, but also worked directly with every other function involved, from design, production engineering, purchase, production control and logistics and many suppliers. We knew that they had other pressing demands for their own resources, so we provided the necessary resources from our own people.

The "impossible" happened!

The unit came in at the same price as its predecessor, on time and with the fastest ramp up we had ever achieved.

We followed every step with regular obeya meetings and used the obeya to engage and inform all related people.

Perhaps the true breakthrough was the realisation that we had the tools, and the ability, to challenge and overcome any previously 'accepted truth.'

As a couple of further examples, when we heard the words "This part is too specialised to be localised" and "We won't be able do all the things needed to change from two shifts to full three shifts and back for just three months without massive losses in performance!" we made a lie out of the 'accepted truths' each time and on many other occasions.

Top management's willingness to commit themselves to the achievement of such challenges and fulfilling their role as champions and supporters in practically helping their people to keep moving forward successfully is truly key. Once ownership is given, it should never be taken away, especially when the owner is at risk of failing. Top management's job is to help them succeed, in whatever way is necessary, and then to celebrate the owner's success.

Back in the day, in previous employment, we used to half jocularly say that any project had the important stages of:

- *Pressure the willing.*
- *Punish the participants.*
- *Reward the uninvolved.*

In Toyota, we knew that if we used the Andon appropriately there was still a risk of failure, but only when everyone at every level had done all they could to ensure timely success.

CHAPTER 32

FINDING THE MISSION

FINDING THE MISSION

During the writing of this book, we have seen that many of the accepted truths, upon which strategic decisions were made by organisations, have been irrevocably changed. Some examples are:

- Effective alternatives to fossil fuels have been developed.
- Cash currency has been largely made obsolete.
- Our impacts upon the environment have become much clearer.
- Technology has made remote working an attractive alternative and challenged the very nature of city centres.
- Autonomous vehicles are no longer a dream.

And within the next few years:

- The race for new medicines will be overtaken by the race for choices which avoid most lifestyle-related illnesses.
- Housing design will integrate with new materials and technology.

In summary, a strategy is an essential element of good organisational management. This, combined with high flexibility and fast reactions, will enable organisations to keep up with most changes.

Is this enough for the organisation which has started to challenge Progressive maturity?

Should such an organisation not be considering what its role in society actually should be, thus allowing its members to widen the scope and depth of their vision to incorporate anticipating and meeting society's future needs?

In other words, to find the mission?

Whether our organisation provides products, services or both, our effectiveness directly relates to how well the organisation is meeting the needs and desires of the societies in which we operate.

For example, if our organisation has a product such as motor vehicles, then our strategies can be to maintain or increase company benefits by finding new markets, more attractive or diverse products, expansion, acquisition or reducing costs or a combination of these.

The Proactive organisation will be doing this within a 5 to 10-year window and periodically adapting the strategy to meet upcoming trends and circumstances.

At the Progressive level, an organisation has resources and top management time to study more widely and deeply the probable future scenarios.

Based upon these findings, the organisation can consider what role it would like to play.

For example, Toyota adopted many different Proactive level strategies. Diversification into building houses, boats and even a small plane. Acquisitions of other Japanese vehicle makers, expanding to America, then Europe, then globally and, of course, continually reducing costs through TPS.

At the same time, back in the 1970s and 80s, the top management were studying the probable longer-term future.

The corporation adopted the mission statement "To make even better cars, to build a future where everyone has the freedom to move."

There was a main outcome:

The global awareness of the environmental impact of fossil fuel-based power was coming to the fore. The conventional petrol engine was under pressure. Electrical cars were hampered in practical application because of battery capacity and recharging infrastructure. So Toyota began developing the hybrid petrol/electric vehicle (the Prius, launched in 1997) which dramatically reduced fuel consumption. At that time, there was no market for such a car. The concept was unknown and actually remained misunderstood for several decades, but the corporation recognised the need and set about creating the desire by undertaking mass production and marketing even though the required volume and technology refinement would mean a period of losses.

More recently, the corporation recognised the issue of fossil fuel and carbon-based energy was much wider.

Battery power is a good interim development, but battery manufacture has its own environmental issues. Renewable energy sources are naturally very unstable and require some method of storing energy for the periods when supply is not enough to meet demand.

A complete and dramatic change was identified; to commercially develop the energy produced by hydrogen-oxygen molecule combination as an energy source.

Producing hydrogen can be done in many ways, including the use of renewable energy. The combination process is safe, silent and produces only water as a by-product. The first commercially produced hydrogen-powered car, the Toyota Mirai, was launched in 2014 with a range of more than 500km.

In 2021, Toyota amended its mission statement: "To attract and attain customers with high-valued products and services and the most satisfying ownership experience."

The broader mission incorporated a specific element which was related to the study of global demographics.

There is a trend for increased longevity, combined with a move away from several generations sharing housing. More and more older people are living separately from their immediate families. Their longevity is not, as yet, accompanied by sustained health and strength, but rather the period of dependency of the aged population is increasing. Toyota began to develop simple and useable robotic support and communication methods which would help the limited capability person in doing some domestic tasks and, at the same time, allow remote relatives and friends to communicate and even help with managing the robotic support. Similar progress was made upon developing more flexible methods of transporting people with limited mobility.

The revised mission also opened the range of opportunities to incorporate the new and exciting possibilities of further developments in artificial intelligence.

The integration of environmentally friendly energy supplies with AI-enhanced living and mobility experiences is being made a reality in the jointly established 'Woven City' located close to Mount Fuji in Japan. Leading corporations, in almost every related field, are taking part in this crucible of experiment and development.

Finding the mission involves many of the same tools as making a strategy. SWOT analysis, in particular, plays an important part in both, but at quite different levels.

The pace of fundamental changes in the priorities, technology, assumptions and possibilities of living will continue to accelerate.

Finding a mission is essential for any organisation which wishes to have long-term sustainability and continued progress.

CHAPTER 33

FROM MISSION TO PRACTICAL PLANS

BUSINESS PLANNING

Turning the mission and subsequent Direction Deployment general statements into concrete and measurable plans is a step often missed in many organisations.

How to know how much resource is needed?

How to know the appropriate size of each step towards the desired condition?

Too often these difficult questions remain unanswered, which makes the task of every level, from board to workforce, very difficult both to justify and to judge.

There is a tool for business planning which Toyota entities use to turn objectives into concrete plans and, in the absence of hearing of an available alternative, I will share it with you.

You may notice many parallel approaches and similar tools to Practical Problem-Solving described in Chapter 6. The logic flow is very similar.

The experience gained in Practical Problem-Solving during the Stabilising and Proactive stages of maturity will be very valuable for senior and top management at this point.

Facilitation of the business planning process often falls to the CEO's corporate office.

STEP 1: DECIDE THE OWNER

In Direction Deployment, Chapter 8, we discussed the need for KPIs to have one leader in the organisation.

Business planning is a higher level of Direction Deployment activity and so the owner will usually be at general manager or director level. This will ensure that the necessary resources can be brought to bear on the subject at every stage of the analysis, planning and delivery. All of the subsequent steps of business planning are the responsibility of the owner.

STEP 2: BREAKING DOWN THE ISSUES

One topic or issue of the organisation's mission may involve many previously, or newly, created performance KPIs.

Breaking down the topic into these KPIs is a vital step for success.

This step needs to be taken with great care. KPIs naturally become targets. Those KPIs which will lead to true improvement and avoid focusing resources and energy upon things which are misleading should be selected.

STEP 3: VISUALISE THE GAP

Identifying the 'ideal condition' starts the process. What is our aspirational performance level for this KPI? For example, 100% customer satisfaction.

Then the current situation for the KPI is added and the gap between actual and ideal calculated.

From then a timescale for achieving the ideal condition is decided.

Over that timescale, the annual progress targets are set.

In general, it is better to set the targets with the largest step in the first year and gradually reducing the yearly incremental improvement targets from then. This follows the natural Pareto principle (80% of the results come from the first 20% of the effort expended). If the improvement activities are well prioritised, the returns for effort will naturally reduce as progress on any topic is made, unless a complete breakthrough is made.

Of course, the target lines can be revisited after more detailed investigation and prioritisation with other KPIs, but it is fundamentally against natural laws and bad practice to have target increments increasing with time.

STEP 4: GATHER THE FACTS

This step often involves investigation and data gathering. To close the gap in performance between ideal and actual, it is often helpful to investigate where losses are happening and by how much.

In the case of customer satisfaction, for example, a history of customer complaints, satisfaction survey scores and survey comments, and customer rejects can usually be categorised into concrete issues. The proportion of losses for each type of cause can also be determined.

At this stage only the major categories may be discernible, but that is enough.

This step is vital for success. I have experienced many important organisations which fall back upon emotional exhortations to employees to improve a KPI, such as safety, customer satisfaction or quality. There is a sense that there is a direct connection between individual good intentions and positive attitudes and improved performance. There is, of course, but seldom one which delivers structured and sustained improvement in customer satisfaction through improved, internal methods and improved and structured two-way communication with the customer.

Slogans are often used. "Customer is number one", "Walk in your customer's shoes","100% customer satisfaction – our aim" and so on. They are very helpful if used as a part of a structured roll out of plans and actions, but merely background 'noise' if not.

This step can take several days of effort. It may seem

expensive at the time, but each minute spent at this stage will deliver multiple times the results versus not taking this time at the beginning.

Also, at this stage, the potential benefits of improving each of the categories of issue begins to be measurable and prioritisation can start.

The relative performance of the types of losses are used to prioritise which of the types need attention and in which order. Using the Pareto principle will help to decide the most beneficial order. The percentage impact line of the Pareto analysis will also provide an excellent way to measure the potential impact of the elements of each plan.

STEP 5: POINTS OF CAUSE

If the subject is important enough to be a KPI, it is very likely that it is already the subject of some form of improvement activity.

Probably, there is already a systematic approach to the subject.

At this point, the current activities and their elements need to be studied versus the actual results and the identified priorities.

Visualising the improvement system or actions in their correct order is very helpful. From this, it becomes possible to grasp which of the systems are working well and which are not delivering their intended benefits.

These are the points of cause which need to be addressed and modified, or reinforced, in order to achieve performance improvement.

STEP 6: MAKE THE PLAN

The previous steps will have provided a number of items to be either further investigated or directly addressed.

The points of cause analysis will have provided how these relate to current activity. At this point, more detailed analysis may be required to find the individual actions to directly impact the KPI.

During the first cycles of experience with this tool, the plan needs only to identify the item to be further investigated, the timing of the investigation, start and completion, and its owner.

Also, the plan should indicate when the investigation and subsequent improvement plans need to be completed in order to meet the business needs.

STEP 7: GAIN CONSENSUS

The outcome of steps 1 to 4 will have resulted in a quite complex action plan which may span several years and involve many organisation functions.

At this point, the owner of the topic has the responsibility for gathering together empowered representatives of all the related functions to go through the business planning document and explain the facts and logic upon which it is based and also the items to be delivered and the actions to be followed. As with Direction Deployment, new information and a more organisation-wide understanding of facts, priorities and resources may well modify the final proposals. After the first cycle of business planning, the majority of the senior management involved will have incorporated this into the earlier steps by ensuring the correct people are represented in them.

STEP 8: AUTHORISATION

It has surprised me many times that this step is missing from business planning. The step is to gather the full top management team together and to formally go through each of the business planning documents the owners have made and to authorise them.

In this step, it is not unknown for a gap in the process to be identified and corrected before work proceeds.

Once again, as with Practical Problem-Solving, the top team should put their own opinions to one side. The fact gathering, analysis and prioritising/planning processes should be confirmed for facts and logic. If these are sound, the plans proposed should be endorsed, even if they seem, on the surface, to be contrary to individual common sense or experience. Only if new information or wider knowledge is available should the owner's conclusions be requested to be revisited.

CHAPTER 34

SUMMARY

SUMMARY

By keeping the two wheels in balance at the forefront of our thinking, our business benefits and our organisation's power grow in parallel.

Taking the maturity levels in the correct order and using each of the tools and their elements in the correct combination, our progress will be sustained into the future and we will continue to grow.

By now, you will have clearly recognised the essential elements of each level of maturity.

From Reactive to Stabilising, we are bringing the organisation under management control and eliminating the disturbance losses our organisation has been experiencing (disturbances of defects, shortages, equipment breakdowns, etc.). In doing so, our methods have developed our people's abilities to prioritise, analyse, countermeasure and standardise. The complete process, from customer order to customer satisfaction, is visible and our policies and principles are known and followed by everyone.

Every step along the way is aligned to our immediate business priorities and delivers business benefits.

The members of the organisation know that management will always immediately step up and support them if they are struggling.

The organisation knows where it is going and by when it will get there.

Profits and customer satisfaction steadily grow.

The organisation is stable and the foundations are laid.

From Stabilising to Proactive, we build upon this foundation.

We introduce ourselves and our people to the concepts

and tools of kaizen and challenge. By implementing and disseminating them, we continually reach new levels of power and performance.

From here, the status quo becomes the thing to be challenged by everyone.

Our people become confident that they can, and are expected to, secure their future by finding and eliminating all forms of waste from their organisation. In doing so, more and more power will be freed up to accelerate even more.

As experience grows, so the sophistication of the tools also grows and a virtuous cycle of never-ending improvement begins.

Management feels confident in selecting levels of challenge previously unimaginable.

Profitability and competitiveness grow and accelerate.

The structure is built and can flex with the ravages of the marketplace and fortune.

From Proactive to Progressive we, as a top management team, have grown our own strength and that of those beneath and around us. We can now spend time deeply considering the future of our organisation, not only in isolation but also as a part of society. What changes and challenges are coming in the medium to long term? What do we need to do to be ready to serve our society when they come?

We have the tools to ensure that the necessary preparation is carried out in good time.

The organisation is flexible and fast acting. Our people can take care of today, we can focus upon the future.

Moving through the stages of maturity is a journey for us in top management to take for ourselves. At each stage we, ourselves, learn by doing first, then bring the rest of our organisation along with us. In this way, the speed of progress and its sustainability will be optimum.

For some of us, the changes to previous priorities, thinking ways and habits will be profound. They were for me. They may be for you and your team.

There will be many frustrations and missteps along the way.

We are no less fallible than anyone else in our organisation and, like them, we will need time and practice to become comfortable with new ways of doing things. Don't beat yourself up if you don't always get it right. No one does. It is celebrating the learning from our mistakes, and in preventing them in the future, which differentiates us and our organisation.

Committing to new methods and principles as a top management team makes progress smoother and less painful. Teamwork really does help, especially if we all promise to administer a swift kick in the pants if we see someone reverting to their old ways!

Remember that it is fine and normal that different parts of the organisation will be at different levels of maturity. Prioritising the business needs, as the guiding force, will automatically make this so. The key point is that each part of the organisation is moving forward all the time.

There will come a critical point at which the number of engaged and powerful people will enable progress to be self-generating, usually during the Proactive development stage. This is when the organisation will start to take your breath away with the things they are doing. This is also when you may begin to feel a little afraid that the organisation might be accelerating almost faster than you can keep up. When the mission, principles and Direction Deployment are well established and your people know how to follow facts and logic, there is little to worry about, except keeping them challenged enough for their continued development.

Excellent people will leave to start their own journey in new pastures. If they leave for advancement or to begin their own organisation, it should be considered a badge of honour. Don't worry, if you have assured that each level is developing the level below them every day, through normal business, there will be excellent replacements for the leavers waiting for their chance to contribute at the next level.

After 50 years in business and 5 years in consultancy, I am delighted to help others to make the journey. It is my dream and my mission.

The Toyota Lean Management Centre in the Toyota Deeside North Wales plant is designed to enable any organisation to go and see first-hand and to be able to question and to learn from Toyota professionals who have earned their spurs by doing it themselves.

There are many other men and women who have made the journey, many directly with organisations that have reached Progressive maturity. Their experience is worth listening to, and they also may even be able to show you the actual thing in action.

All anyone will ask of you is to listen and look with humility and an open mind. Put self-esteem and pride away, they are a deadly poison.

Pride comes in the progress and development of others and watching their confidence and ability grow. Esteem comes from ensuring that their progress and development is appreciated by everyone and anyone who may be able to contribute to their future level of contribution.

Look for the leader that unfailingly allows his or her people to share their contribution with you directly, who openly explains failures and shares the learning. That is the person who will add the most value to your organisation.

Through the whole journey, keep at the very front of everything that you do:

BOTH WHEELS MOVING IN BALANCE

ACKNOWLEDGEMENTS

There are too many people to list that have made significant impact upon my learning over three decades. I will only mention those people who spent their resources and time helping a struggling and limitedly competent general manager to make the first and most difficult part of the journey towards company president and CEO in the Toyota Europe organisation.

MUTSUKATSU KANEDA

My first coordinator in my concurrent role of inspection operations manager in Toyota UK and who must have had the most frustrating time of his career trying to teach me. *(His nickname for me was Ishi Atama san – Mr. Stone Head!)*

SHINICHI SASAKI

My first boss in Toyota UK. He directed many of the initial Toyota domestic support members to overcome their horror at my methods and spend their precious time teaching me. *(Sasaki san went on to become one of Toyota's corporate vice presidents but has never lost contact with any of the people who worked with him.)*

SIR ALAN JONES

The first manufacturing director of Toyota UK who went on to be the first local managing director. I was fortunate to work with Alan for almost 30 inspiring years.

Printed in Great Britain
by Amazon